THE TALE OF
THE CAMPAIGN OF IGOR

THE TALE OF
THE CAMPAIGN OF IGOR

A RUSSIAN EPIC POEM
OF THE TWELFTH CENTURY

Translated by
ROBERT C. HOWES

W· W·NORTON & COMPANY · INC · *New York*

Contents

Acknowledgments

I owe a special debt of gratitude to Vladimir Nabokov, several of whose courses on Russian literature I attended at Cornell University from 1948 to 1950. His brilliance as a teacher and his personal kindnesses to me will always be cherished.

I also wish to record my special thanks to Professor Robert Hoopes who, when chairman of the Department of English at Oakland University, encouraged me to continue my work on *Prince Igor*. I am especially grateful as well to Marian Wilson for her historical and literary acumen, her invaluable assistance in the preparation of the manuscript, and her unfailing encouragement. Thanks are also due to Barbara J. Biallas, who prepared the map of Igor's campaign.

Robert C. Howes
Rochester, Michigan
May 1973

THE TALE OF
THE CAMPAIGN OF IGOR

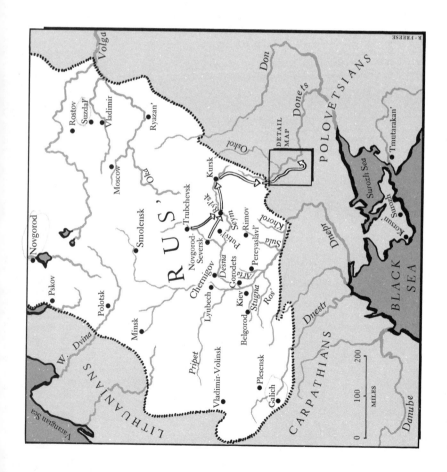

The Campaign
of Prince Igor

Introduction

In the year 6576 [1068].[1] Foreigners came to the Russian Land. Many Polovetsians. Now Izyaslav, and Svyatoslav, and Vsevolod went out against them to the L'to. And it being night, they went out against each other. Now, because of our sins, God set the pagans against us and the Russian princes fled and the Polovetsians were victorious.
—*Lavrent'yevskaya Chronicle*

In the second half of the twelfth century Russia was ruled by various members of the princely family that would later trace its origin to Ryurik the Varangian (or Viking), who, according to tradition, came to rule the Slavs of the Ladoga and Novgorod region in 862. The veracity of this tradition and the real role of Ryurik remain uncertain and continue to be topics of both serious research and heated debate among Russian historians. It is quite clear, however, that by about 880 one of Ryurik's successors, the powerful and energetic Viking warrior-merchant Oleg the Wise, had imposed his control—and a semblance of unity—upon a number of the Slavic peoples living along the great trade route (known as the Great Water Route) between the Baltic Sea and Constantinople. Oleg and two of his successors, princes Igor and Svyatoslav, warred with their neighbors, on several occasions even forcing the haughty Byzantines to enter into trade agreements with the barbarians of Rus'.

In the latter part of the tenth century the unity of the eastern Slavs was strengthened through the adoption of Byzantine Christianity by the ruling class of Rus' under the leadership of Grand Prince (later Saint) Vladimir. With the reign of Yaroslav the Wise (1015–1054) the unity and prosperity of Kievan Rus' seemed secure. Yaroslav, a strong, able, and reasonably enlightened prince, maintained order along the Great Water Route from the Varangians to the Greeks, defeated the principal enemy from the steppes (the Pechenegs), and furthered the development of the city of Kiev as one of the leading European cities of the time. Before he died, Yaroslav wrote a will in which, apparently hoping to avoid such a

1. For information about the Russian chronicles, see p. 53. Until the time of Peter the Great (1682–1725), the Russians calculated dates from the Creation which, following the Greeks, they placed 5508 years before the birth of Christ. Hence, A.D. 1068 corresponds to the year 6576 (5508 plus 1068).

1

conflict as that which preceded his own accession to the throne, divided Rus' among his five surviving sons and one grandson. This action unfortunately had the opposite result; contention among the princes was renewed, the prize being the "golden throne of Kiev," the senior city of Rus'.

Kiev, on the Dnieper near the border of forest and steppe, was the most important city of Old Russia. The prince of Kiev was considered the senior prince of the House of Ryurik; he usually had at his disposal a strong military force, and his control of the middle Dnieper and much of the Great Water Route added to his importance. It was his duty to defend all Rus' against invaders and to keep open the trade route.

Kiev dominated Russia from the ninth century until about the middle of the twelfth century. By this latter date the political and economic fragmentation of Rus' had reached such proportions that new centers of power were beginning to emerge, centers that would eventually replace Kiev in power and importance. These were the Vladimir/Suzdal' Land in the northeast between the Volga and Oka rivers, the great northern trading city of Novgorod with its vast territories, and the Galich/Volynya Land to the west. Yet the idea lingered that all Rus' was one and that it was the common patrimony of all the princes of the House of Ryurik. Moreover, the fiction of Kiev as the dominant city of Rus'—the Mother of Russian Cities —was long in dying.

If the lack of princely unity weakened Kievan Russia from within, the steppe nomads threatened her from without. The Polovetsians (called Polovtsy, Cumans, or Kipchak Turks) had been moving into the steppes north of the Black Sea since the 1050s, replacing the older enemies of the Russians, the Pechenegs, who had been decisively defeated by the Russians during the reign of Yaroslav the Wise. The *Ipat'yevskaya Chronicle* reports that in 1055: "That same year came Bulush' with the Polovetsians and Vsevolod made peace with them and they returned to their own land." —This incursion was into the Pereyaslavl' Land and probably as far as the Dnieper River. In 1068 the Russians were defeated by the Polovetsians on the Al'ta (L'to) River.

In the late eleventh and early twelfth centuries Kiev was threatened by a powerful alliance of Polovetsians under the leadership of two khans, known to the Russians as Bonyak the Mangy and Sharukan the Old. This threat was so great that, under the leadership of the brilliant Vladimir Monomakh (d. 1125) and his son Mstislav the Great (d. 1132), the princes of Rus' temporarily set aside their differences and dealt the Polovetsians several serious defeats. But with the death of Mstislav and the apparent subsidence of the danger from the steppes the princes of Rus' returned to their bickering and internecine wars, while the feudal fragmentation of Kievan Russia continued apace. The enmity between two of the most gifted and energetic of Russian princely lines—the descendants of Vladimir Monomakh and the descendants of his cousin Prince Oleg of Chernigov—well illustrates the irreconcilability of the antagonisms among the princes.

Between 1136 and 1170 several events took place that illustrate the danger Kiev faced. In 1136 a serious uprising in Novgorod foreshadowed the establishment of a republic dominated by boyars and wealthy merchants, in that great city near the northern terminus of the Great Water Route. The uniting of the Black Cowls (*Chernyye klobuki*, a Turkic people) in the region of the Ros' River southwest of Kiev, and the organization of two Polovetsian political units in the steppes—the Western and Eastern alliances—also boded ill for Kiev. Furthermore, Kiev was being weakened by the gradual decline of the Great Water Route, a result of the reorientation of Byzantine trade to the West during the Crusades. From about 1170 the Eastern alliance of the Polovetsians, under the leadership of Khan Konchak, renewed its pressure on the southeastern border of Rus'.

The Polovetsians were nomads. Living in movable camps, they were cattle raisers and warriors. The enmity between them and the Russian farmer, artisan, and trader was similar to the classic enmity between the Chinese and the nomadic peoples living beyond the Great Wall. But in the case of Russia there was no Great Wall and there was no strong emperor standing at the head of a highly developed, centralized state apparatus. In Russia there were only open plains and warring princes.

A curious entry in the *Ipat'yevskaya Chronicle* for the year 1159 indicates that as early as that date the lands along the middle Dnieper were already becoming deserted as a result, at least in part, of the ravages of the Polovetsians. When Prince Izyaslav Davidovich of Chernigov succeeded to the Golden Throne of Kiev in 1157, he granted the city of Chernigov and seven other towns to his cousin, Prince Svyatoslav Vsevolodovich of Novgorod-Seversk. When, in 1159, Grand Prince Izyaslav planned a campaign against Galich, he called upon Prince Svyatoslav for aid. When Svyatoslav refused, Izyaslav replied: "If God grants that I succeed in Galich, then do not complain to me when you go crawling from Chernigov [back] to Novgorod." The Chronicle reports that Svyatoslav, greatly angered by these words, said: "My lord, you see my humility. How much of that which is mine have I foregone, not wishing to spill Christian blood or bring my patrimony to ruin. I received Chernigov and 7 empty cities: Moravsk, Lyubech, Orgoshch, Vsevolozh, and in them are [only] dog keepers and Polovetsians."

Excellent horsemen and experienced fighters, the Polovetsians would make yearly forays into the southeastern borderlands of Kievan Russia. Burning villages and grainfields, besieging and sacking towns and carrying off captives to be sold as slaves to Arab, Greek, or Italian merchants, they menaced the peaceful population of Rus' for almost two centuries. Their very name must have struck terror in the hearts of Russians.

Yet the Polovetsians never completely defeated the Russians: they seemed to be satisfied with the booty from their raids against Rus'. On the other hand, the Russian princes could not unite to bring an end to the Polovetsian threat. Although it is true that by about 1200 there had developed an uneasy truce among the Russians and the nomads of the steppes, the Polovetsian threat did not completely disappear until it was replaced by the much more serious threat of the Mongols. But the discord among the princes of Rus' remains the darkest page in the history of Kievan Rus'.

In 1185 *two* Russian princes were referred to in the chronicles as Grand Prince of Kiev. The first and most powerful was Prince Ryurik Rostislavich of Smolensk. The great grandson of Vladimir Monomakh, Ryurik neither resided in nor reigned in Kiev. (Seven times during his life he gained Kiev for himself; twice he returned it voluntarily to its former prince.) The other Grand Prince of Kiev was Svyatoslav Vsevolodovich. A grandson of Oleg of Chernigov, Svyatoslav was a member of the princely family that had contended so stubbornly with the Monomashichi (descendants of Vladimir Monomakh) for supremacy in Kiev. He had ruled in Novgorod-Seversk and then in Chernigov. In 1178 he moved to Kiev, where he ruled in collaboration with Prince Ryurik of Smolensk and other Rostislavichi.

THE STORY OF IGOR'S CAMPAIGN

Now at this time a junior prince, Igor Svyatoslavich, ruled in Novgorod-Seversk, a lesser city on the Desna, northeast of Chernigov. Igor, born in 1150, was the grandson of the famous Oleg of Chernigov and the cousin of Grand Prince Svyatoslav of Kiev. Prince in Novgorod-Seversk since 1178, Igor was an active participant in the internecine wars of his time. In 1180 he and other Ol'govichi (Oleg's descendants), with Polovetsian allies, invaded Smolensk and fought against Prince David Rostislavich. Then, with Khans Konchak and Kobyak, Igor moved against Kiev in support of Grand Prince Svyatoslav, whose claim to the throne of Kiev was not secure. Although successful in driving Grand Prince Ryurik from Kiev, Igor and his Polovetsian allies were defeated subsequently.

The chronicler, reporting the battle on the Chertoryya (a tributary of the Dnieper, near Kiev), writes: "Now the Polovetsians were fleeing before the Russian troops [of Grand Prince Ryurik and] many were drowned in the Chertoryya, and others were captured, and others were slaughtered. Now seeing the Polovetsians defeated, Igor and Konchak forthwith leapt into a boat and fled to Gorodets [and] to Chernigov."

Three years later, in 1183, Prince Igor and Prince Vladimir Glebovich of Pereyaslavl' undertook a campaign against the Polovetsians. But there was a disagreement between the two princes as to whose forces should lead the way, and Vladimir, angered, turned and plundered Igor's principality of Novgorod-Seversk.

In 1183 Grand Prince Svyatoslav inflicted a serious defeat on the Polovetsians, taking prisoner Khan Kobyak. The Ol'govichi did not participate in this victory. But Igor and his brother Vsevolod, Prince of Trubchevsk and Kursk, hearing of the Polovetsians' defeat, undertook a campaign of their own against the Polovetsians, toward the Donets River. This undertaking was a failure.

Early in 1185 the "accursed and godless and thrice-cursed Konchak, with a multitude of Polovetsians" invaded Rus'. Grand Princes Ryurik and Svyatoslav met the invaders on the Khorol River and on March 1 "God . . . gave the victory to the Russian princes." (It is here that the account of Igor's campaign from the *Ipat'yevskaya Chronicle*, given in full following p. 53, begins.)

According to the Chronicle Igor had wanted to participate in the campaign to the Khorol but was unable to do so because of the tardy arrival of the runner with the news of the campaign. But on April 23, 1185, Prince Igor, without having consulted the senior princes, Svyatoslav of Kiev and Ryurik of Smolensk, set out with his son Vladimir (who was fifteen at the time), his brother Vsevolod, and his nephew Svyatoslav of Ryl'sk, on a campaign into the Polovetsian steppes intending to "lay down my head or / Drink with my helmet from the Don." (It is true that Igor did consult Prince Yaroslav of Chernigov, who contributed his boyar Olstin Oleksich and some Turkic mercenaries to Igor's army.)

There was apparently opposition to this campaign among members of Igor's retinue. On May 1, 1185, there was an eclipse of the sun, which the *Nikonovskaya Chronicle* describes: "A Portent. That same year, in the month of May, on the 1st day, there was a portent in the sun; it was very dark, and this was for more than an hour, so that the stars could be seen, and to men's eyes it was green, and the sun became as the [crescent] moon, and from its horns flaming fire was emitted; and it was a portent terrible to see and full of horror." Although the Russians interpreted this phenomenon as an evil omen, Igor insisted that the campaign continue, saying, "No one knows the mysteries of God. God is the maker of this sign and of the whole world. And whether that which God does to us is for good or for ill, this too we shall see" (*Ipat'yevskaya Chronicle*).

In the first battle, on Friday, May 10, 1185, the Russians were victorious over what was apparently merely a rather small scouting detachment of Polovetsians. Igor now urged retreat, saying, according to the Chronicle: "Lo, God with His strength has inflicted a defeat on our enemies and [has given] us honor and glory. Lo, we saw the Polovetsian armies that were many. But were they all gathered here? Let us ride the night . . ." Igor may well have sensed the impending disaster. But his nephew Svyatoslav (who was only nineteen) objected, noting that his men were tired and that if the main body of Russians were to retreat, some of his men would be left behind on the road. Igor's brother, "Wild Ox" Vsevolod, the most dashingly heroic personage in *Prince Igor*, sided with Svyatoslav, and the Russians pitched camp for the night.

Prince Igor's estimate of the situation had been correct. The following morning, Saturday, Polovetsian troops "began to appear like a forest." The Russians, alarmed, held a council of war. Some argued for retreat, but now Igor insisted that they stand their ground, saying: "If we flee we shall ourselves escape, but we will leave the black people [the common foot soldiers]. That will be a sin against us from God, having betrayed them. Let us go: we shall either die or be alive in one place." So the princes and voivodes (officers) dismounted and went into battle against the Polovetsians.

All day they fought and into the night. When Sunday morning dawned the battle was still raging. And then the Turkic mercenaries, the Koui, panicked and began to fall back. Igor, who had been wounded in the arm and was on his horse, set out at a gallop to rally them. Thinking that they, having caught sight of him, were indeed returning to the battle, Igor galloped back toward his own men. Unfortunately, the Koui did not return to the fight but continued their retreat; only one man, according to the Chronicle a certain Mikhalko Georgiyevich, turned back. When Igor was within an arrow's flight of his own men he was taken prisoner. At this moment—one of the most dramatic in the story—Vsevolod was seen by Igor, surrounded by the enemy and fighting fiercely. Believing all was lost, Igor "asked for his soul's death that he might not see his brother fall."

But neither prince was killed. The Polovetsians carried the day and decisively defeated the Russians, taking many prisoners, including Igor, Vsevolod, and Igor's son Vladimir.

Following their defeat of the Russians, the Polovetsians decided to counter the Russian attack with an invasion. They entered Rus' with two armies: the one commanded by Khan Gza struck into the Posem'ye (the area along the Seym' River in the Chernigov Land); the other, under Khan Konchak, invaded the Principality of Pereyaslavl', southeast of Kiev. Although both armies caused much destruction and laid waste many Russian districts, the result, typical of all the Polovetsian raids, was not conclusive. Konchak besieged Pereyaslavl', where .Prince Vladimir Glebovich—grandson of the terrible Yuriy Dolgorukiy of Suzdal' and apparently a favorite of the chronicler—was seriously wounded in a heroic defense of his city. Unable to capture Pereyaslavl', Konchak retreated, sacking the town of Rimov on his way back to the steppes.

Grand Prince Svyatoslav did not hear of Igor's campaign until he chanced to stop at Novgorod-Seversk on his way to Kiev from Karachev, where he had been raising men for another campaign against the Polovetsians. Displeased that Igor had undertaken such a campaign, Svyatoslav proceeded to Chernigov; here he learned of Igor's defeat and capture. The Chronicle relates that Svyatoslav, upon hearing the news, wiped away his tears and said: "O my beloved brothers, and sons, and men of the Russian Land! God has given it to me to weaken the power of the pagans; but you, not restraining your youthfulness, have opened the gates to the Russian Land. May the Lord's will be done in all things. As I have grieved for Igor, so now I lament for Igor, my brother, even more."

Grand Prince Svyatoslav had taken measures to counter the impending Polovetsian invasion of Rus'. He sent his sons Oleg and Vladimir into the Posem'ye, the area along the Seym' River that was especially open to attack from the steppes. He sent word to Prince David of Smolensk, who had apparently intended to participate in the campaign, calling upon him to come immediately with his army. David started down the Dnieper but halted at Trepol', a town south of Kiev near Pereyaslavl'. The grand prince's brother, Prince Yaroslav of Chernigov, did nothing. The Chronicle reports that he, having gathered his troops, waited in Chernigov. It was at this time that the two-pronged Polovetsian invasion began. Vladimir, the valiant defender of Pereyaslavl', appealed to Svyatoslav and to Ryurik and David: "Lo, the Polovetsians are at my gates. Help me!"

David and his Smolensk men turned back, refusing to go farther; but Svyatoslav and Ryurik set out against the Polovetsians, who retreated, sacking Rimov as they went. The Russians did not pursue them into the steppes but returned home. Igor and his fellow Russians remained in captivity.

According to the Chronicle Prince Igor, early in his captivity, became deeply troubled by feelings of guilt. The prince, blaming himself for the disastrous campaign, said: "I remembered my sins before the Lord my God: how I caused many killings and [much] bloodletting in a Christian land; how I showed no mercy to Christians, but took by storm the city of Glebov. . . . I was not worthy to live. And lo, now I see the vengeance of the Lord my God. Where now is my beloved brother? Where now is the son of my brother? Where is the child to whom I gave birth? Where are the boyars of my council? Where are my brave nobles? Where are my men of the line? . . . Lo, the Lord has repaid me for my lawlessness and for my evil. This day my sins have descended upon my head. . . . But O Master, O Lord my God, do not reject me utterly! But as Your will is, O Lord, so is Your mercy toward us, Your servants" (*Ipat'yevskaya Chronicle*).

Igor felt that it would be dishonorable for him to try to escape: "For the sake of glory I did not flee then [during the battle] from my retinue, and now I shall not flee ingloriously." But at least two of Igor's counselors, the son of a chiliarch (commander of a thousand men) and the prince's groom, advised otherwise, feeling that the Polovetsians, returning unsuccessful from their campaign, might in frustration kill the prisoners, especially the princes and voivodes for whom sufficient ransom had not been forthcoming. (The eighteenth-century Russian historian Tatishchev wrote that because the chiliarch's son was the lover of Khan Toglyy's wife, he heard from her of plans to kill the Russians and thereupon alerted Igor's groom. According to the *Ipat'yevskaya Chronicle*, both the chiliarch's son and the groom warned Igor of the danger.)

Fortunately for Igor, a Polovetsian named Lavor (or Ovlur)— Tatishchev says he was a Christian—offered to help Igor escape. One evening when Igor's guards were drinking koumiss (fermented mare's milk), the prince stole from his tent to meet Lavor, who had two horses ready on "the other side of the Tor [River]," and made his escape. Khans Gza and Konchak pursued Igor but failed to recapture either him or Lavor. Crossing the Donets River, the two men arrived at the town of Donets. Igor then went to Kiev, where he was greeted with great joy by the two grand princes, Svyatoslav and Ryurik.

Such, in brief, is the account of the campaign, captivity, and escape of Prince Igor of Novgorod-Seversk. The campaign had not been decisive; in fact, it was much less important historically than a number of similar campaigns undertaken by Russian princes (including Igor himself) in the twelfth century. Yet this comparatively insignificant campaign was to be immortalized by an epic poem, probably written in the year 1187 by a contemporary, perhaps one of Igor's retinue.

COMMENTS ON THE POEM

In dividing the poem into sections and giving each section a title, I follow I. A. Novikov, who has translated *Prince Igor* into modern Russian.

1. *The Beginning of the Song: About Boyan*

The author starts the poem by asking rhetorically if he should not sing of the sorrowful campaign of Prince Igor in ancient words such as those that might have been used by the bard Boyan. The historicity of this bard has not been positively determined, although it is believed that such a poet-singer was to be found in the retinue of most princes of Kievan Rus'. It is probable that a renowned bard named Boyan did live and that he flourished at the court of Svyatoslav Yaroslavich in the third quarter of the eleventh century.

The author of *Prince Igor* speaks of Boyan as a wizard whose "thought would range . . . like a grey wolf across the land, / Like a blue eagle against the clouds." He would sing of the old wars and of the great heroes of earlier days. His fingers, as he plucked the strings of the gusli (an ancient musical instrument), are compared to ten falcons released upon a flock of swans. But the author of *Prince Igor* does not intend to imitate Boyan, although he has been doing just that, but will tell his story "in the manner of a tale of today."

2. *Igor Prepares for the Campaign*

In describing the preparations for Igor's campaign, the poet again mentions Boyan ("O Boyan, you nightingale of olden times!") and cannot resist offering two passages as they might have been sung by the famous bard. In one of these passages he conveys beautifully the air of tense martial expectancy that preceded the opening of the campaign against the Polovetsians.

Horses neigh beyond the Sula;	Komoni rzhut' za Suloyu;
Glory rings out in Kiev.	Zvenit' slava v Kyyeve.
Trumpets blare in Novgorod;	Truby trubyat' v Novegrade,
Banners flutter in Putivl'.	Stoyat' styazi v Putivle.
And Igor awaits his dear	Igor' zhdet mila
brother Vsevolod.	brata Vsevoloda.

3. *The Campaign Begins*

This section begins with a brilliant monologue by Igor's brother, Prince Vsevolod of Trubchevsk, describing the readiness of his men:

> And Vsevolod, the Wild Ox, said to him:
> "My only brother, my only Bright Light,
> You, Igor, and I are both sons of Svyatoslav;
> Saddle, brother, your swift steeds,
> For mine are ready, they are
> Already saddled at Kursk;
> And my men of Kursk are skilled warriors;
> Under trumpets were they swaddled,
> Under helmets were they cradled,
> And they were suckled at the end of a spear.
> They have travelled all the paths,
> The ravines to them are known.
> Their bows are drawn tight,
> And their quivers are open,
> Their sabres are sharp,
> And they ride like grey wolves
>   across the plains,
> Seeking for themselves honor
> And for their Prince, glory."

The army sets out. Ill omens abound: the eclipse of the sun, the "moaning night" that awakens the birds "with its ominous sounds," the "howl of wild beasts," the screaming of Div, a supernatural bird of ill omen. Yet Igor is not deterred; he leads his men on. It is here that the first passionate note of love of country is heard: "O Russian Land, you are / Already behind the hill!"

4. *The First Day of Battle, a Night of Rest and Another Battle*

On the first day of battle the Russians are victorious, taking many prisoners and much booty; but dawn of the second day foreshadows the coming tragedy:

> The second day, very early,
> The blood-red sky heralds the dawn.
> And black clouds move in
> From the sea to cover the Four Suns.
>
> And in these clouds the
> Blue lightning glitters.
> There will be great thunder
> And rain will fall like arrows
>   from the Great Don.
> And spears will be blunted here,
> And sabres will be dulled here,

Against the helmets of the Polovetsians,
On the river Kayala,
Near the Great Don.

O Russian Land, you are
Already behind the hill!

The battle is joined again. The Chronicle reports that in the midst of the battle Igor caught sight of his brother Vsevolod. The poet sings:

O Wild Ox Vsevolod!
You stand ahead of all,
Flinging arrows at the enemy,
Striking their helmets with your
　　　　kharalug [steel] swords.
Wherever, Ox, you gallop,
Your golden helmet flashing,
There lie pagan Polovetsian heads.
Slashed are the Avar helmets
By your sabres of cold steel,
O Wild Ox Vsevolod!
What to such a one are wounds,
O brothers,
Who thinks not of life,
Or of honor,
Or of the town of Chernigov,
Or of the golden throne of his father,
Or of the ways of his Sweet Desire,
　　　　the Beautiful Glebovna!

With the magnificent description of Wild Ox Vsevolod (could the poet have been a member of this prince's retinue?) the account of the battle is abruptly interrupted. We have not yet been told its outcome. (Note that this is also a high point in the account of the battle given in the *Ipat'yevskaya Chronicle*; see p. 57.)

5. *Memory of the Wars of Oleg Svyatoslavich*

Russian tradition retained the memory of Vladimir Monomakh (Grand Prince of Kiev, 1113–1125) as the very model of a Christian prince, one who fought to defend Rus' against its pagan foes and who strove to put an end to the internecine wars of the princes. The principal competitor of Monomakh was his cousin, Oleg Svyatoslavich of Chernigov; and the struggle between these two princes and among their descendants (the Monomashichi and the Ol'govichi) was the epitome of princely struggles in Kievan Russia.

The author of *Prince Igor* is a gifted and passionate apologist for his heroes Igor and Vsevolod, grandsons of Oleg of Chernigov, but

12 · *The Tale of the Campaign of Igor*

he does not hesitate to condemn Oleg, who "forged discord with his sword and sowed arrows throughout the land."

The poet refers to Oleg as "Gorislavich" and through this epithet characterizes this prince, and others like him, as "sons of sorrowful renown."[2]

Prince Oleg Svyatoslavich—"progenitor of an entire dynasty of rapacious Ol'govichi, friend of Polovetsian khans, and instigator of internecine wars"—was one of the five sons of Svyatoslav Yaroslavich, Prince of Chernigov, and, from 1173 to 1176, Grand Prince of Kiev.[3] From a miniature of Svyatoslav and his family that has been preserved in the *Izbornik Svyatoslava*, a collection of miscellaneous writings, dated 1073, the three older sons of the prince, among whom was Oleg, are depicted as young men with beards. From this fact, and on the basis of other information, we assume that Oleg was born about 1050.

The young Oleg may have learned of the exploits and wars of the Russians from the bard Boyan, who was probably the court singer of his father Svyatoslav. He probably read yet another *Izbornik*, that of 1076, which contains a large number of aphorisms directed to the mighty and the weak, to the prince and the common man: "Do not admit just any man to your home but guard yourself against the evildoer." "Fear the prince with all your might." "Bright is my goodness and light is my burden." Yet we may assume that Prince Oleg was influenced most of all by the baleful example of his father, who, in the words of the chronicler, "began to remove his brothers" from their princely thrones. Svyatoslav participated in the betrayal of Prince Vseslav of Polotsk in 1067 (see below), and in 1073 he conspired against his own brother Izyaslav, Grand Prince of Kiev. The latter fled to Poland and Svyatoslav became Grand Prince.

In 1076 Prince Oleg and his cousin, Vladimir Monomakh, were sent to Poland to assist King Boleslaw in his struggle against the Czech king, Vratislav. When the Poles and the Czechs made peace, with the Czech king paying Boleslaw a contribution of 1,000 *grivna* of silver,[4] the Russian princes laid siege to the city of Glogow, claiming that the honor of their fathers and of their land had not been satisfied. They plundered Czech lands for four months and

2. It is dangerous to place much faith in the explanation of names. However, if Ivan is derived from the Greek Ioannis which, in turn, is from the Hebrew Yehōkhānān 'gift of God'; if William comes from the French Guillaume and is related to Wilhelm 'helmet of resolution'; and if Yaroslav signified something akin to 'of bright renown'; then Gorislav would mean 'of sorrowful renown,' and Gorislavich 'son of sorrowful renown.'

3. This and much of the information on Oleg that follows is based on the chapter "The 'Gorislavichi' Princes and the Kiev Uprising of 1113," by B. A. Rybakov, in B. A. Rybakov, ed., *Istoriya SSSR* [History of the USSR], First Series, Vol I (Moscow: Izdatel'stvo "Nauka," 1966).
4. The *grivna* was the basic monetary unit of Kievan Rus'. It was a bar of silver weighing about one pound.

were induced to depart only after having themselves received 1,000 *grivna* of silver.

When his father became Grand Prince of Kiev in 1073, Prince Oleg was given Rostov Land in the northeast of Rus' as his patrimony. Not satisfied, he also claimed Chernigov as his patrimony. For a time he resided in Chernigov when his uncle Vsevolod was ruling in that city; but the same year, 1077, he fled to Tmutarakan' on the Straits of Kerch, where his brother Roman was prince. (This was the "handsome Roman Svyatoslavich" of whom Boyan sang in Part 1 of the poem.)

In Tmutarakan' Oleg and another cousin, Prince Boris Vyacheslavich, entered into an alliance with the Polovetsians, and "Oleg and Boris brought the pagans against the Russian Land and they went against Vsevolod with the Polovetsians" (*Ipat'yevskaya Chronicle*). Oleg seized Chernigov, but a coalition of princes under Vsevolod and Grand Prince Izyaslav defeated him at the battle of Nezhatina Niva (Unharvested Grain Field) on October 3, 1078. During the "wicked slaughter" Grand Prince Izyaslav and Prince Boris were both killed, but Oleg escaped to Tmutarakan':

> And the search for glory
> Led Boris Vyacheslavich, brave and young,
> To his death, and laid for him
> A shroud of green grass
> To the shame of Oleg!

In 1079 Oleg's brother, Prince Roman of Tmutarakan', was killed by the Polovetsians and Oleg was seized by the Khazars and carried off to Constantinople. He remained in the Byzantine Empire for four years, probably not as a prisoner for all that time. He spent two of those years on the island of Rhodes and married a Greek noblewoman.

Returning to Tmutarakan' in 1083, Oleg took savage revenge on the Khazars and drove from the city two lesser Russian princes who had recently seized it. For ten years thereafter Oleg is not mentioned in the chronicles. He probably remained in Tmutarakan' during these years.

In 1092 and 1093 the political and economic situation in Rus' was extremely unsettled. The reigning grand prince, Vsevolod, was growing old and was unable or unwilling to control the lesser princes and greedy retainers, whose exactions from the helpless people of Rus' seemed more cruel with each passing year. The grand prince himself shared in these ill-gotten gains. To add to the people's suffering, there was a terrible drought in 1092.

Grand Prince Vsevolod died in 1093 and his son, Vladimir Monomakh, was the logical choice to succeed him. But the boyars of

Kiev feared Monomakh, and the throne went to his cousin, Svyato-polk Izyaslavich, whose father had been killed at Nezhatina Niva. In the words of Rybakov, Svyatopolk, "a poor military leader, a clumsy politician, arrogant, greedy for money, suspicious and cruel, . . . quickly turned all against him and by his policies deepened the crisis."

As recorded in the *Ipat'yevskaya Chronicle*: "Svyatoslav came to Kiev. The Kievans came out to meet him with a bow and they received him with joy. And he sat on the throne of his father and his uncle. At this same time Polovetsians came to the Russian Land. Hearing that Vsevolod had died they sent emissaries to Svya-topolk concerning peace. Now Svyatopolk did not take counsel with the senior retinue of his father and uncle but took counsel with those who had come with him. Seizing the emissaries, he thrust them into a dungeon. Now hearing of this, the Polovetsians began to make war. And many Polovetsians came and they entered Torchesk city. Now Svyatopolk, hearing of the Polovetsians, sent asking for peace. But the Polovetsians did not want peace and they set out about the country, warring."

Svyatopolk's men advised him to send to his cousin Vladimir Monomakh for help. Vladimir gathered his men together and sent to his brother Rostislav in Pereyaslavl', ordering him to come to the aid of Grand Prince Svyatopolk.

Vladimir and his men went to Kiev and he and his cousin Svya-topolk quarrelled, and "settling their quarrel they kissed the cross to one another [*i.e.*, swore allegiance to one another]. And the Polovetsians were warring throughout the land. And the thoughtful men said to him [them?]: 'Why is there discord between you while the pagans destroy the Russian Land? You must make peace and go now against them, either in peace or in war.' Now Vladimir wanted peace but Svyatopolk wanted war. And Svyatopolk and Vladimir and Rostislav set out for Trepol' and they came to the Stugna [River]." After further disagreement, the armies crossed the Stugna which "was then flooding greatly."

The Polovtsy attacked Svyatopolk's men first. The prince held firm but the enemy "broke his army," which fled, followed by Svya-topolk. Now the Polovtsy turned on Vladimir and there was a fierce battle. "And Vladimir and Rostislav and their warriors fled and they ran to the Stugna River. And Vladimir and Rostislav were fording the river and Rostislav began to drown before the eyes of Vladimir. And he wanted to support his brother and he almost drowned himself. And thus did Rostislav, son of Vsevolod, drown. Now Vladimir forded the river with a small retinue, many of his army had fallen and [many of] his boyars fell here. And arriving on the other side of the river, weeping for his brother and for his retinue, he went to Chernigov, very sorrowful."

The Polovetsians roamed at will throughout southern Russia. In the words of a contemporary, quoted by Rybakov: "All the cities and villages were deserted. If we walk across the fields where herds of horses, sheep, and oxen used to graze, we see all is barren; grain fields are overgrown with weeds, and only wild beasts live here." The Polovetsians "carry off to their tents, to their people, large numbers of Christian folk; people suffering, sorrowing, subject to torments, benumbed by the cold, tortured by hunger and thirst, with swollen faces, blackened bodies, and inflamed tongues; they wander about a strange land, without clothing, barefoot, tearing their feet on the sharp, prickly weeds."

Some elements among the upper classes attempted to end this intolerable situation, but the princes like Oleg Svyatoslavich continued to pursue their own selfish goals: Oleg invaded Rus' at the head of a Polovetsian army, besieged and captured Chernigov where Monomakh was residing, and allowed his Polovetsian troops to plunder his native Chernigov Land.

For the next three years Oleg protected the Polovetsians, refusing to wage war against them in company with his cousins Svyatopolk and Vladimir. Eventually the Russian princes attacked Oleg and, led by Monomakh, pushed back the armies of Khans Tugorkan and Bonyak. Oleg was forced to negotiate with his cousins.

The council of the princes held in Lyubech (November 1097) attempted to regularize the relations among the princes. It was agreed that Rus' would be governed by the princely families but that in times of external danger Rus' would be as one. This agreement had little effect.

In the years immediately following the congress of the princes at Lyubech, enmity between Grand Prince Svyatopolk and Prince Vladimir Monomakh grew. It culminated in the famous incident of the blinding of Vasil'ko, a prince accused of conspiring with Monomakh against the grand prince. This incident signaled the beginning of a fierce civil war, with Monomakh and Oleg of Chernigov allied against Svyatopolk. The Polovetsians, Hungary, and Poland, as well as innumerable Russian princes, were drawn into this war which was finally concluded at another meeting of the princes at Vitichev in 1100. At this conference Prince Vladimir Monomakh served as the chief accuser of those held responsible for the blinding of Vasil'ko.

One senses that Oleg was becoming old and tired. He does not appear to have played as dominant a role in these last wars as one might expect. He died in Chernigov in 1115. The last three months of his life were taken up by a dispute with Vladimir Monomakh—now Grand Prince of Kiev—over the location of the tombs of Saints Boris and Gleb.[5]

Such, in brief, was the career of Prince Oleg "Gorislavich" of Chernigov. An energetic and gifted man, his unscrupulous conduct must have contributed greatly to the suffering of the people of Rus'.

> And so it was in the days of Oleg Gorislavich:
> Civil wars were sown and grew,
> And in them perished
> The patrimony of the grandsons of Dazhbog;
> In these princely wars
> The lives of men were cut short.

> And then throughout the Russian Land,
> Seldom did the plowmen
> Shout to one another.
> But often did the crows caw,
> Dividing among themselves the corpses,
> And the jackdaws would speak in their own tongue,
> As they flew out after prey.

6. The Defeat of the Russians and the Great Sorrow of the Russian Land

The author resumes the account of the battle that was interrupted by Part 5. On the third day of the battle the Russians are defeated and all nature mourns for them. How could such a tragedy have happened? Because the Russian princes had contended too selfishly with one another:

> For brother said to brother:
> "This is mine, and this too is mine."
> And the princes began to say of small things:
> "This is great."

When the people at home hear of Igor's defeat they are overcome with grief: "And Sorrow gallops through the Russian Land"; and Kiev "groaned in its sorrow, / And Chernigov in its misfortune." The poet laments that the two princes, Igor and Vsevolod, have reawakened the threat from the steppes, a threat that Grand

<hr/>

5. Boris and Gleb were the first Russians to be canonized, and a devout cult devoted to their veneration as martyrs arose soon after their deaths. Both were victims of strife between their brothers, Yaroslav, Prince of Novgorod, and Svyatopolk, Prince of Turov, as to who would succeed their father, Grand Prince Vladimir I (d. 1015), on the Golden Throne in Kiev. Gleb was murdered by Svyatopolk's hired assassins; Boris fell victim to two Varangians, whose orders came from either Svyatopolk or Yaroslav (it is not certain which). Boris and Gleb offered no resistance to their murderers, and they are remembered as symbols of Christian non-violence, brotherly love, and forgiveness, while Svyatopolk is known in Russian history as "the Accursed."

Prince Svyatoslav had weakened by his successful expeditions against the Polovetsians.

7. *The Dream of Svyatoslav and His Talk with the Boyars*

This section contains one of the most intriguing episodes in the poem: the mysterious dream of Grand Prince Svyatoslav. The prince, speaking to his boyars, relates his eerie dream, with its overtones of sorrow and death:

> "On the evening of that night
> They clothed me," he said,
> "In a black shroud, on my cedar bed.
> They poured me blue wine mingled with bitterness.
> From empty Polovetsian quivers
> They sprinkled great pearls upon my breast,
> And they treated me tenderly.
>
> "And across the golden ceiling
>   of my tower chamber
> There is no ridge beam.
> And from evening through all the night,
> Grey crows cawed
> There at Plensk, along the river,
> Where used to be the Kiyan thickets,
> And then they flew off to the Blue Sea."

Unfortunately, the last four lines of the dream sequence are defective and their translation is uncertain.

The boyars of Svyatoslav explain his dream by saying that he is distracted by grief ("Grief has taken your mind prisoner, O Prince."). They then tell him of the defeat of Igor and of the pagans' rejoicing.

8. *The Golden Word of Svyatoslav and His Appeals for Princely Unity*

In this section is found the "Golden Word" of Svyatoslav and his appeal for princely unity.[6] The grand prince laments Igor's defeat even while upbraiding him for recklessness in undertaking such a serious enterprise without consulting the senior princes:

> "Your brave hearts were forged
>   from strong steel
> And tempered in daring.
> But what have you done
>   to my silver-grey hair!"

6. The expression "golden word" must have been familiar to educated Russians of the twelfth century who had heard the homilies, in Slavic translation, of the great father of the church St. John Chrysostom ("golden-mouthed"). The adjective *golden* is found in a number of works of the age, used in the sense of "eloquent, fine, beautiful."

Svyatoslav now refers to his age (he was probably in his sixties). Comparing himself to a falcon that has lost its feathers in moulting yet is still capable of driving the other birds high into the sky to protect its nest (another favorite figure of the poet), he bemoans the fact that the other princes will not aid him: "But this is the evil: / The princes give me no aid; / The times are turned inside out." (Note that the *Ipat'yevskaya Chronicle* reported that Prince David of Smolensk, although standing at Trepol' south of Kiev, refused to move against the Polovetsians after Igor's defeat.)

If the "Golden Word" of Svyatoslav ends at this point—and there is uncertainty as to exactly where it does end—the author of *Prince Igor* now continues Svyatoslav's lament: calling on some of the most powerful princes by name, he asks why they are unwilling to aid their brother Igor. In one of the most celebrated passages, Grand Prince Vsevolod Big Nest of Vladimir is apostrophized:

> O Grand Prince Vsevolod!
> Have you not thought to fly from afar,
> To guard the Golden Throne of your fathers?
> For you can splash the Volga with your oars
> And lade the Don with your helmets.

Another interesting passage concerns Prince Yaroslav of Galich, the father of Igor's wife. He, too, is called upon to war against the Polovetsians:

> Prince Yaroslav Osmomysl of Galich!
> High do you sit on your gold-bossed throne.
> You propped the Hungarian mountains
> With your iron armies . . .
>   *   *   *
> Fear of your might flows throughout the lands.
> You force the gates of Kiev,
> And from the Golden Throne of your fathers
> You shoot at the sultan in a distant land.
> So, lord, shoot at Konchak, the pagan slave, . . .

The section closes with a bitter denunciation of Grand Prince Yaroslav the Wise (or perhaps the grandsons of Yaroslav) and "all the grandsons of Vseslav":

> O Yaroslav, and all the grandsons of Vseslav!
> Lower your banners,
> Put away your blunted swords!
> For you have already fallen from the glory
>   of your grandfather!
> For with your sedition you began to bring
> The pagans into the Russian Land,
>   the patrimony of Vseslav.
> In your discord violence came
>   from the Polovetsian Land!

The mention of the grandsons of Vseslav, Prince of Polotsk, intro-
duces the next part of the poem.

9. *The Song of Vseslav*

This section concerns Vseslav Bryachislavich, the wizard Prince
of Polotsk. His life epitomizes the long struggle between the princes
of Polotsk and the descendants of Yaroslav of Kiev. The author of
Prince Igor recounts briefly some of Vseslav's more daring exploits:
his seizure of Kiev, his escape from that city, his taking of Novgorod, and his defeat by the Yaroslavichi at the battle of the Nemiga
River in 1067. This battle was, in the poet's words, another terrible
example of the futility and tragedy of the princely wars:

> On the Nemiga
> They scattered heads like
>   sheaves of grain,
> And threshed them with
>   kharalug flails;
> On the threshing floor
>   they placed men's lives,
> And winnowed their souls
>   from their bodies.
>
> On the bloody shores of the Nemiga
> The sowing was to no good:
> They sowed the bones of Russian sons.

The section concludes with a contrast between Grand Prince
Vladimir of Kiev (ruled *ca.* 980–1015) who ruled wisely a unified
Rus', and two of his descendants, Ryurik and David of Smolensk,
both of whom were deeply involved in the internecine wars of the
twelfth century.

10. *The Lament of Yaroslavna*

In this justly famous section, Yaroslavna, the wife of Igor, grieves
for the fate of her wounded and captive husband. The princess
sings from the wall of Putivl', the city of her stepson, Prince Vladimir Igorevich. Longing to be with Igor, she sings, at dawn:

> "I shall fly," she says,
> "As a cuckoo, along the Danube.
> I shall wash my sleeves of beaver
> In the river Kayala.
> I shall cleanse the bleeding wounds
> On the mighty body of my prince."

Yaroslavna then addresses three of the mightiest natural forces of the Russian Land: the Sailing Wind, the Dnieper River (Son of Renown), and the Thrice-Bright Sun.

Weeping, she asks the Wind why he blew so strongly and drove the pagan arrows against her husband's men.

> Is it not enough for you,
> Flying on high beneath the clouds,
> To rock the ships upon the Blue Sea!
> Why then, O Lord, did you scatter
> My happiness about the feather-grass!

Of the Dnieper she recalls, weeping, that he had once cradled the boats of Grand Prince Svyatoslav in a successful campaign against the Polovetsians; "Then cradle, O Lord, my Beloved to me." Lamenting that the Sun is warm and beautiful for all, Yaroslavna cries:

> Then why, O Lord, did you send
> Your hot rays onto the troops
> Of my Beloved!
> On the waterless plain,
> Why did you warp their bows with thirst
> And close their quivers with sorrow!

(Solov'yev remarks that on the second day of battle the Russians were already suffering badly from a shortage of water.)

11. *Igor's Escape*

This section tells of Igor's escape and his safe return to Rus'. "And God shows Prince Igor the way / From the Polovetsian Land, / To the Russian Land, / To the Golden Throne / of his fathers."

Igor is aided by Ovlur (Lavor in the Chronicle), a Polovetsian, who obtains horses and flees with the prince. If God "shows Prince Igor the way," it is the natural forces of the Russian Land that give him practical assistance: he hides in the rushes, he hides in the mists, the Donets River "cradles" him on its waves and spreads green grass for him on its "silver shores."

Khans Gzak and Konchak pursue Igor and Ovlur but fail to recapture them. Gzak suggests that they shoot "the little falcon" (Igor's son, Prince Vladimir); Konchak counters this suggestion by proposing that they "entangle the little falcon / With a beautiful maiden." In his reply, which is the only touch of humor in the entire poem, Gzak demonstrates both his understanding of human nature and his political acumen:

> If we entangle him with a beautiful maiden.
> We will have neither the little falcon

Nor the beautiful maiden;
And the birds will make war against us
On the Polovetsian Plain.

12. *Final Praise for Igor and His Men*

In this brief conclusion the poet praises Igor and his men. The
Russian Land is again happy, now that the prince has returned
safely. Igor rides to Kiev, "up to the Borichev Slope / To the Holy
Mother of God Pirogozhchey." The concluding lines are a paean to
the young princes:

> Glory to Igor Svyatoslavich,
> To Wild Ox Vsevolod,
> And to Vladimir Igorevich!
> Health to the princes
> And to their retinues,
> Who fight for Christians
> Against the armies of the pagans!
> Glory to the princes and their retinues!

NATURE AND RELIGION IN THE POEM

The author of *Prince Igor* must have been very familiar with the
fauna and flora of his country. Many animals are named in the
poem, though fewer plants and flowers are mentioned. Other natural phenomena—sun, wind, clouds, lightning, rivers, plains—also
play important roles. Not many trees are mentioned, but this is natural because Igor's campaign was into the steppes. A mere listing of
the animals named is impressive: wolves, horses, wild oxen (probably aurochses, similar to bison), foxes, squirrels, leopards, "wild
beasts," ermines, and snakes. The list of birds is even longer: eagles,
swans, falcons, nightingales, ravens or crows, hawks, jackdaws,
cocks, cuckoos, white ducks, geese, golden-eyes (sea ducks), sea
gulls, black ducks, magpies, and woodpeckers.

The poem abounds with metaphors involving animals and birds.
Boyan's thoughts ranged "like a grey wolf across the land / Like a
blue eagle against the clouds." Boyan was a "nightingale of olden
times." The carts of the retreating Cumans screeched at midnight
like "a flock of startled swans." Igor is a mother bird who protects
her brood from harm. Yet in the next line the Russians are wolves,
then eagles, then foxes.

Throughout the poem Prince Vsevolod is a Wild Ox. Prince
Vseslav of Polotsk (the wizard) is a wolf, Yaroslavna is a cuckoo,
the Polovetsian is a black raven. Individual Russians are almost

invariably falcons; collectively they are a "nest." What poetic force there is in these lines!

Oleg's brave nest slumbers
In the field;
    Far has it flown!
Yet it was not born
    to suffer wrong
From hawk, or from falcon,
Or from you, black raven,
    Pagan Polovetsian!
	Dremlet ve pole Ol'govo
	Khorobroye gnezdo.
	    Daleche zaletelo!
	Ne bylo ono obide
	    porozhdeno,
	Ni sokolu, ni krechetu,
	Ni tebe, chernyye voron,
	    Poganyy Polovchine!

Igor and his men are falcons, even in captivity:

> But the falcons' wings
> Have been brought to the ground,
> By the swords of the pagans,
> And the falcons themselves
> Are bound in bonds of steel.

Many other passages could be cited, but they are best appreciated in the context of the poem.

Most of nature—animals, birds, phenomena such as the sun and the rivers—usually, but not always, works to the benefit of the Russians. The eclipse of the sun is, of course, a warning of the tragedy that awaits Igor, although he fails to heed it. Yaroslavna chides the wind for having driven the arrows of the enemy against the troops of Igor. Similarly, she upbraids the Dnieper River and the sun for failing to aid the Russians, for in fact aiding their enemies. The overall tone of Yaroslavna's lament indicates that it is unnatural for the forces of nature to work against the Russians. Incidentally, the passage in which Yaroslavna addresses the sun is one of the most beautiful and poetically effective in the poem:

O Bright and Thrice-Bright Sun!
For all you are warm and beautiful!
Then why, O Lord, did you send
Your hot rays onto the troops
Of my Beloved!
On the waterless plain,
Why did you warp their bows
    with thirst
And close their quivers with sorrow!
	Svetloye i tresvetloye solntse!
	Vsem teplo i krasno yesi!
	Chemu, gospodine, prostre
	Goryachyuyu svoyu luchyu
	Na lade voi!
	V pole bezvodne
	Zhazhdeyu im luchi
	    spryazhe,
	Tugoyu im tuli zatche!

Once Igor and Ovlur succeed in escaping from the Polovetsian camp, it is the natural forces of the Russian Land that aid them. Particularly the Donets River, with the spirit of which Igor converses, offers protection to the fleeing prince. It is fitting that Igor escapes on a horse and is protected and comforted by one of the great rivers of Russia. Among the Russians the horse has traditionally been man's best friend. And it is difficult to exaggerate the role of the great rivers in both the history and the folklore of Russia. Of particular interest is Igor's apostrophe to the Donets in which he praises that river for saving the life of a Russian prince, unlike the

Stugna River which many years before had been the instrument of death for another prince.

Turning to religion in the poem, it is obvious that pagan beliefs play a much greater role than do Christian. Boyan the Bard is called "grandson of Veles" (the Slavic god of cattle and wealth and perhaps the patron of singers). As Igor and his men set out into the Wild Plain (*dikoye pole*, an ancient term for the danger-infested region south of the area of firm Russian control), we are told that

> Div screams from the top of a tree,
> Bidding the Unknown Land be on guard:
> The Volga, the Pomor'ye, and Posul'ye, and
>   Surozh, and Korsun',
> And you, Idol of Tmutarakan'!

Div was apparently a supernatural bird of ill omen, perhaps related to the griffin. She was an ally of the enemies of Rus' and warns them of approaching danger. Later in the poem, when Svyatoslav's boyars are speaking of Igor's defeat, they say: "Now shame has replaced glory / And thundering violence has stunned freedom; / Div has plunged to earth." It is as though the evil bird had plunged to earth and participated in the defeat of the Russians.

Stribog, god of the winds, is another Slavic deity mentioned: "Lo the winds, grandsons of Stribog, / Blow as arrows from the sea / Against the brave troops of Igor." It is of interest that the prevailing spring winds in southern Russia are from the south-southeast.

Other pagan Slavic gods mentioned are Dazhbog, probably a sun god and the progenitor of the Russian race; Khors, a sun god; and Troyan, whose identity is uncertain. Some scholars believe that Troyan, at least in the adjectival form in which it appears in *Prince Igor*, is derived from the name of the city of Troy. Others believe it derives from the name of the Roman emperor Trajan. George Vernadsky in *Kievan Russia* argues that Troyan was an epithet of Svarog, the Slavic sky god, and means "the father of the three sons"; i.e., Dazhbog, Khors, and Stribog.

Personification, a figure used quite often in *Prince Igor*, is also suggestive of paganism. Thus, Obida (wrong, injustice, offense) is pictured as a maiden with swan's wings:

> For now, O brothers,
> A time of sorrow has come,
> And desolation covers our troops.
> Obida has risen up
> In the army of the grandson of Dazhbog.

> As a maiden she stepped forth
> Into the Troyan Land;
> With her swan's wings
> She splashed the Blue Sea by the Don.

> And, splashing, she banished
> The times that were fat.

A few lines further on, Lamentation (*Karna*) and Sorrow (*Zhlya*) are personified:

> O far has the falcon flown,
> Killing birds, to the sea!
> But Igor's brave army will not be raised!
>
> Lamentation shrieks for it,
> And Sorrow gallops through the Russian Land,
> Hurling fire at the people from flaming horns.

And of course in Yaroslavna's lament the Sun, the Dnieper, and the Wind are personified, as is the Donets River during Igor's escape. Furthermore, the legend of the wizard Prince Vseslav is a non-Christian semi-religious belief of a type that lingered on in Russia for centuries after Christianization.

Christian references are few. Several churches are mentioned: Saint Sofiya's in Kiev, Saint Sofiya's in Polotsk, and the Church of the Holy Mother of God Pirogozhchey in Kiev. But these references are coincidental. Note that the reference to Saint Sofiya's in Polotsk occurs in the midst of the tale of the wizard Prince Vseslav.

God is mentioned only twice: "And God shows Prince Igor the way / From the Polovetsian Land / To the Russian Land," and "Not the clever one, / Nor the skillful one, / Nor skillful bird, / shall escape the judgment of God." It is quite probable that these references are to the Christian God rather than to an unidentified pagan deity. There is no reference to Jesus in the poem. Neither is there a reference to the martyred princes Boris and Gleb, whose murder in 1015 by order of their brother, Svyatopolk the Accursed, would have served as an excellent example of the evil of princely strife. No saints are named ("Saint Sofiya" means "Holy Wisdom"). The Virgin Mary appears only as the name of a church. Such ubiquitous accoutrements of the Christian warrior as icons and crosses are conspicuously absent. The overall impression is that the author of *Prince Igor* was at heart a pagan, despite the occasional Christian allusions in the poem. This is especially marked in comparison with the account of the campaign in the chronicles.

PATRIOTISM AND THE HERO IN THE POEM

Prince Igor can be analyzed according to four subjects or themes: (1) the campaign, including the defeat, capture, and escape of Igor;

(2) laments (for Igor's defeat, for the princely wars); (3) appeals for princely unity; (4) brief sections concerning Boyan the Bard. If laments and appeals are combined into one general category, the *patriotic*, then this category makes up almost three-fourths of the poem.

The central idea of the poem is that of Rus' as a nation whose interests transcend all others. In their internecine wars and their refusal to aid Igor, the princes of Russia, in theory, violated a trust. To the Christian ideologue, the princes failed to carry out two of the primary duties of a prince: defense of the Christian state and church and protection of the Christian folk. Although the concept of the Christian prince is not present in the epic poem, it is stressed in the account of Igor's campaign in the Chronicle.

There are many passages in the poem that illustrate the theme of patriotism. Perhaps the one in which the author cries out passionately to Grand Prince Ryurik Rostislavich and his brother Prince David of Smolensk serves as well as any:

You, wild Ryurik and David!	Ty, buy Ryuriche i Davyde!
Is it not your golden helmets	Ne vayu li voi zlachenymi
That are floating in blood?	shelomy
Is it not your brave warriors	Po krovi plavasha?
Who, wounded by tempered	Ne vayu li khrabraya druzhina
sabres,	Rykayut aky tury raneny,
Scream like wild oxen on an	Sablyami kalenymi na pole
unknown plain!	neznayeme!
Step then, lords, into your	Vstupita, gospodina,
golden stirrups,	v zlata stremen',
For the wrong of our times,	Za obidu sego vremeni,
For the Russian Land,	Za zemlyu russkuyu,
For the wounds of Igor,	Za rany Igorevy,
the wild son of Svyatoslav!	buyego Svyatslavicha!

No single character dominates the poem; there is no hero in the Classic sense. Although Igor is occasionally described in heroic terms, on balance he is not presented as a particularly brave or dashing leader. His self-seeking recklessness colors his courage and determination. Vsevolod, the Wild Ox, is described in the battle scene as a fearless warrior who is prepared to die for the cause. But this picture is fleeting. Grand Prince Svyatoslav is viewed as a wise and saddened older man who grieves for the misfortunes of his younger relatives yet recognizes their shortcomings. Prince Oleg of Chernigov, Prince Yaroslav of Galich, and Prince Vseslav of Polotsk are described in intriguing but not heroic terms. If there is a real hero in *Prince Igor* it is the unknown author of the poem, whose fearlessness, morality, and artistic genius place him in the forefront of the great men of early Russia.

THE TEXT OF THE POEM

Sometime between 1788 and 1792 Count A. I. Musin-Pushkin, a bibliophile and amateur of Russian antiquities, acquired a number of old documents from Archimandrite Ioil of the Monastery of the Saviour in Yaroslavl'. Among them was an untitled manuscript concerning the campaign of Prince Igor against the Polovetsians in the spring of 1185.[7] Although it was thought that this group of documents dated from the sixteenth century, Musin-Pushkin later wrote that he believed the manuscript of the Prince Igor tale was written in a script characteristic of the late fourteenth or early fifteenth centuries. Several copies of this manuscript were made, including one for Empress Catherine the Great.

The first printed edition of the poem, including the old Russian text and a translation into modern Russian, appeared in 1800. The work of Musin-Pushkin, the historian Karamzin, and two other scholars, this first printed edition contained a number of errors.

When Musin-Pushkin's Moscow house burned during the Napoleonic invasion of 1812, his priceless manuscript collection, including the original manuscript of *Prince Igor*, was destroyed. The "Catherine Copy" of the poem was preserved, although unfortunately it too contains a number of obvious errors. Working on the basis of the "Catherine Copy" and the first edition of 1800, scholars have reconstructed the original text. Nevertheless, there remain several defective and disputed passages in the poem.

Who was the author of the tale of Igor's campaign, and when was it written? The authenticity of the poem has long been a matter of serious debate among slavicists. The majority opinion holds that the poem is genuine, that it was indeed written in the late twelfth century, perhaps by a participant in the ill-fated campaign of 1185.[8] Whatever the truth may be, there is no doubt that the *Tale of the Campaign of Igor* is one of the great masterpieces of world literature and that it fairly breathes the spirit of Kievan Rus'.

7. The Russians call the poem *Slovo o polku Igoreve*, which I have translated *The Tale of the Campaign of Igor*. The word *slovo* in this context might also be translated "song" or "lay".

8. The poem was probably written in 1187. Because Prince Vladimir Glebovich of Pereyaslavl' and Prince Yaroslav Osmomysl of Galich are both treated as living persons in the poem and because they both died in 1187, a later date seems unlikely. An earlier date is not possible because the author included Prince Vladimir (Igor's son) among the princes returning from Polovetsian captivity. Igor did not come home until autumn 1187.

Although the identity of the poet remains unknown, there is considerable evidence in the poem that he was a partisan of the Ol'govichi. Perhaps he was the bard of Grand Prince Svyatoslav Vsevolodovich himself.

THE TALE OF
THE CAMPAIGN OF IGOR

1

The Beginning of the Song: About Boyan

Would it not be fitting, brothers,
To begin with ancient words
The sorrowful tale of the campaign of Igor,
 Igor Svyatoslavich.

Now let us begin this song   5
In the manner of a tale of today,
And not according to the notions of Boyan.

Now the wizard Boyan,
If he wanted to make a song to someone,
His thought would range through the trees;   10
It would range like a grey wolf across the land,
Like a blue eagle against the clouds.

His words would recall the
Early years of princely wars:
Then he would release ten falcons   15
Onto a flock of swans;
The first swan to be touched,
It would be the first to sing:
To old Yaroslav, to brave Mstislav,
Who cut down Rededya before the   20
Armies of the Kasogians,
To the handsome Roman Svyatoslavich.[1]

Now Boyan, brothers, would not
Release ten falcons
Onto a flock of swans,   25
But his magic fingers would
He place on the living strings,
And they themselves would
Sound forth praises to the princes.[2]

2

Igor Prepares for the Campaign

Then let us begin, brothers,   30

1. Yaroslav the Wise was Grand Prince of Kiev from 1015 to 1054. The duel between Prince Mstislav Vladimirovich and the Kasogian warrior Rededya is recounted in the "Primary Chronicle" under the year 1022. Prince Roman Svyatoslav-ich died fighting the Polovetsians in 1079.

2. Bards such as Boyan accompanied their songs by plucking the string of the *gusli*, an old Russian psaltery, similar to a zither.

This tale from old Vladimir[3] to the present-day Igor,
Who armed his thoughts with fortitude
And sharpened his heart with manliness,
And, filled with the spirit of war,
Led his brave troops   35
Against the Polovetsian Land
   For the Russian Land.

O Boyan, you nightingale of olden times!
When you trilled the glory of these armies,
Darting as a nightingale about the tree of thought,   40
Flying in your mind against the clouds,
As you wove a song of glory
To days of yore and present days,
Loping along the Troyan path,[4]
Across the plains and into the mountains.   45

Then the song to Igor, grandson of Oleg,
Would go like this:
   "It is not a storm that carries the falcons
     across the broad plains;
   Flocks of ravens flee to the Great Don."[5]   50

Or your song, Wise Boyan, grandson of Veles,[6]
Might go like this:
   "Horses neigh beyond the Sula;
   Glory rings out in Kiev.
   Trumpets blare in Novgorod;   55
   Banners flutter in Putivl'.
   And Igor awaits his dear brother Vsevolod."[7]

3

The Campaign Begins

And Vsevolod, the Wild Ox, said to him:
"My only brother, my only Bright Light,
You, Igor, and I are both sons of Svyatoslav;   60
Saddle, brother, your swift steeds,
For mine are ready, they are
Already saddled at Kursk;
And my men of Kursk are skilled warriors;

---

3. St. Vladimir, who "baptized all Rus' " in the tenth century.

4. Troyan may have been a pagan god of the Slavs. (See above, p. 23) "Troyan's path" signified a great distance. Boyan, a wizard, was able to transport himself to distant places.

5. Perhaps the falcons are the Russians and the ravens the Polovetsians.

6. Veles, the god of cattle and wealth, was perhaps the patron of poets and singers.

7. The Sula is a river. Putivl' is a city south of Novgorod-Seversk. Vladimir, son of Prince Igor, was prince in Putivl'. Vsevolod Svyatoslavich, brother of Igor, was prince of Trubchevsk and Kursk.

Under trumpets were they swaddled, 65
Under helmets were they cradled,
And they were suckled at the end of a spear.
They have travelled all the paths,
The ravines to them are known.
Their bows are drawn tight, 70
And their quivers are open,
Their sabres are sharp,
And they ride like grey wolves
    across the plains,
Seeking for themselves honor 75
And for their Prince, glory."

Then Igor looked up at the bright sun,
And saw that from it all his troops
Were covered with darkness.[8]
And Igor said to his retinue: 80
"O, brothers and friends,
It is better to die than be slaves.
So, brothers, let us mount our swift steeds,
And take a look at the Blue Don."

Desire to taste the Great Don 85
Flamed within the Prince's heart,
And hid from him the meaning of the sign.

"I wish," he said, "to break
My spear with you, O men of Rus',
At the [far] end of the Polovetsian plain. 90
I shall lay down my head or
Drink with my helmet from the Don."

Then Prince Igor set his foot in the golden stirrup
And rode out into the open plain.

The sun barred his way with its darkness; 95
The moaning night awoke the birds
With its ominous sounds;
There rose the howl of wild beasts;
Div[9] screams from the top of a tree,
Bidding the Unknown Land be on guard: 100
The Volga, the Pomor'ye, and Posul'ye, and Surozh, and Korsun',
And you, Idol of Tmutarakan'![1]

---

8. There was an eclipse of the sun, an ill omen, on May 1, 1185.
9. Div, a supernatural bird of ill omen and an enemy of the Russians, here warns the Polovetsians that the Russians approach. Div is equated with the griffin, "a fabulous animal having the head and wings of an eagle and the body and hindquarters of a lion. Believed by the Greeks to inhabit Scythia and to guard its gold" (*Oxford Universal Dictionary*). The root *div* 'wonder,' 'miracle' in Russian, is cognate with Latin *daemon* and Greek *daimon*, "an evil being of superhuman nature."
1. The word *pomor'ye* means the area

And the Polovetsians by untrod paths
Flee to the Great Don;
Their carts screech at midnight   105
Like, say, a flock of startled swans.

Igor leads his troops towards the Don;
Like a mother bird he keeps them from harm;
Like wolves they court danger in the ravines,
Like eagles screaming over the bones of dead animals;   110
The foxes make their way behind red shields.[2]

O Russian Land, you are
Already behind the hill!

The night was long in falling.
Slowly the light of the sunset faded   115
And dark mist covered the plain.[3]
The nightingales fell quiet
And the call of the ravens was heard.
The men of Rus' barred the great plains with their red shields,
Seeking honor for themselves,   120
And for their Prince, glory.

4

The First Day of Battle
A Night of Rest and Another Battle

From early morning of the fifth day,
They trampled under foot the army of pagan Polovetsians.
And, sowing the field of battle with their arrows,
They carried off the beautiful Polovetsian maidens,   125
And with them, gold, and silken cloth,
And thick red and violet velvet, with ornaments.

1. The word *pomor'ye* means the area along a sea (here the Black Sea); Po-sul'ye is the land along the Sula River; Surozh, or Sudak, was a city in the Crimea; Korsun' was Khersones, formerly a Greek colony in the Crimea. The Idol of Tmutarakan' was a huge stone woman venerated by the Polovetsians. Originally it may have been one of the mysterious stone statues carved by the Scythians, or even a Greek lighthouse.
2. The meaning of this stanza is obscure and there are many interpretations. Part of the difficulty stems from the fact that the original manuscript has no punctuation, which makes the phrasing debatable. If my interpretation is correct, the wolves and eagles and foxes are the Russian warriors whom Igor is trying to protect.
3. The word translated "dark mist" is *mgla*; whereas the word used earlier ("Then Igor looked up at the bright sun/ And saw that from it all his troops were covered with darkness" and "The sun barred his way with its darkness") is *t'ma*. Both words are found in modern Russian and both have strong suggestive connotations: *mgla* can mean "twilight," "darkness," "a shroud of fog, dust, smoke," etc.; *t'ma* means "darkness," "ignorance," "cultural backwardness," "100,000 or any huge number."

And with horse cloths, and capes, and cloaks,
They began to lay roads
Across the swamps, across the muddy places.   130
This they did with all
The precious brocades of the Polovetsians.

The crimson banner,
The white pennon,
The crimson horse-tail ensign,   135
And the silver lance:
All—to brave Svyatoslavich.[4]

Oleg's brave nest[5] slumbers
In the field; far has it flown!
Yet it was not born to suffer wrong   140
From hawk, or from falcon,
Or from you, black raven,
    Pagan Polovetsian!

And Gzak flees like a grey wolf;
Konchak, following him, heads for the Great Don.[6]   145

The second day, very early,
The blood-red sky heralds the dawn.
And black clouds move in
From the sea to cover the Four Suns.[7]

And in these clouds the   150
Blue lightning glitters.[8]
There will be great thunder
And rain will fall like arrows
    from the Great Don.
And spears will be blunted here,   155
And sabres will be dulled here,
Against the helmets of the Polovetsians,
On the river Kayala,[9]
Near the Great Don.

4. These four items were captured by the Russians and presented to their prince. The crimson horse-tail ensign was probably the later *bunchuk* of the Turks, "the tail of a horse or of an Indian ox, on a decorated staff, used . . . as the symbol of the rank and power of the pashas" (Dal').

The use of the patronymic alone (Svyatoslavich, instead of Igor Svyatoslavich) suggests affectionate familiarity.
5. Oleg's brave nest was the descendants of Prince Oleg Svyatoslavich of Chernigov, grandfather of Igor.
6. The two Polovetsian khans, Gzak and Konchak, fled before the Russians.
7. The Four Suns were Igor, his brother Vsevolod, his son Vladimir, and his nephew Svyatoslav.
8. The verb *trepeshchut'*, translated "glitter," was seldom used of lightning. Perhaps, as Adrianova-Peretts suggests, this is a metaphor for the glitter of armor and weapons in the coming battle, much the same as thunder, rain, and wind are used in lines to follow.
9. Igor's army will be defeated at the Kayala, "river of regret" or "river of mourning." The existence of such a river in the area of Igor's campaign is doubtful. Vasmer relates the name to the Turkic word *kajaly*, "rocky," and believes that the association of the word with "regret" and "mourning" is based on popular etymology.

O Russian Land, you are   160
Already behind the hill!

Lo the winds, grandsons of Stribog,[1]
Blow as arrows from the sea
Against the brave troops of Igor.
The Earth hums a warning,   165
The rivers run muddy,
And dust covers the fields.
The banners speak:
   The Polovetsians come from the Don,
   And from the sea,   170
   And from all sides
   They encircle the Russian troops.
The devils' sons have sealed off the steppe
   with their shouts,
And the brave Russians have barred it   175
   with their red shields.

O Wild Ox Vsevolod!
You stand ahead of all,
Flinging arrows at the enemy,
Striking their helmets with your kharalug swords.[2]   180
Wherever, Ox, you gallop,
Your golden helmet flashing,
There lie pagan Polovetsian heads.
Slashed are the Avar helmets[3]
By your sabres of cold steel,   185
O Wild Ox Vsevolod!
What to such a one are wounds,
O brothers,
Who thinks not of life,
Or of honor,   190
Or of the town of Chernigov,
Or of the golden throne of his father,[4]
Or of the ways of his Sweet Desire,
   the Beautiful Glebovna![5]

1. Stribog was the god of the winds among the heathen Russians.
2. The Turkic word *kharalug* meant "steel." Probably the swords used by the Russians at this time were of European manufacture.
3. By the late sixth century the Avars, a people of Turkic origin mingled with other ethnic groups, had built a powerful state centering in the Pannonian Plain (modern Hungary). They subjugated the Slavs and exacted tribute from the Eastern Empire. Pepin and Charlemagne destroyed their power and they all but disappeared from history. The "Primary Chronicle" tells of the harsh rule of the Avars over the Dulebs (a Slavic tribe) in the Carpathian region. The chronicler writes that even in his day there was the saying, "They disappeared like the Avars."
4. Prince Vsevolod was one of "Oleg's brave nest." Vsevolod's father Svyatoslav had ruled in Chernigov.
5. Glebovna, 'daughter of Gleb.' Prince Vsevolod's wife was Olga, daughter of Prince Gleb Yur'yevich of Pereyaslavl'. Her brother was Prince Vladimir Glebovich of Pereyaslavl' ("this good Vladimir [who], wounded and suffering, rode into his city and wiped away the sweat for his fatherland"). See below, p. 59.

5

Memory of the Wars of Oleg Svyatoslavich

Gone is the age of Troyan,   195
And passed are the years of Yaroslav.
Gone are the wars of Oleg,
   Oleg Svyatoslavich.[6]

Now Oleg forged discord with his sword
And sowed arrows throughout the land: 200
He would step into his golden stirrup
In the town of Tmutarakan';
And Vsevolod, son of Yaroslav old and great,
Would hear that sound;
And Vladimir each morning   205
Would stop his ears in Chernigov.[7]
And the search for glory
Led Boris Vyacheslavich, brave and young,
To his death, and laid for him
A shroud of green grass   210
To the shame of Oleg!

And from that same Kayala
Svyatopolk bade them carry his father
Between Hungarian pacers,
To Saint Sofiya in Kiev.[8]   215

And so it was in the days of Oleg Gorislavich:[9]
Civil wars were sown and grew,
And in them perished
The patrimony of the grandsons of Dazhbog;[1]
In these princely wars   220
The lives of men were cut short.

6. Concerning Prince Oleg Svyatoslavich, see Introduction, pp. 11–16.

7. Adrianova-Peretts suggests that the "sound" that Vsevolod (father of Vladimir Monomakh) would hear when his nephew Oleg started out in war ("stepped into his golden stirrup") was the actual sound of warlike preparations and rumors. Vladimir Monomakh, remembered as a peacemaker, would cover his ears so as not to hear. Can this suggestion that Monomakh was ineffectual, or even cowardly, be another indication that the author of the poem was a bard of the Ol'govichi?

The meaning of the following lines is explained on p. 13.

8. Svyatopolk was the son of Izyaslav Yaroslavich, Prince of Kiev, who was killed in the battle of Nezhatina Niva. The son ordered his father's body car-ried on a litter slung between two horses to the Cathedral of Saint Sofiya in Kiev.

The word *Kayala* here may be a copyist's error. If not, the poet is comparing the battle of Nezhatina Niva with the battle in which Igor and Vsevolod were defeated, the battle he is preparing to describe.

9. The use of the nickname Gorislavich, instead of the usual patronymic Svyatoslavich, refers to the vicissitudes of Oleg's life and is apparently a play on words. If Svyatoslavich means "son of one who is bright in holiness," then Gorislavich means "son of one who is bright in sorrow" or in "misfortune."

1. Dazhbog was one of the pagan Slavic gods associated with the sky and the sun. He was considered a progenitor of the Russian race.

And then throughout the Russian Land,
Seldom did the plowmen
Shout to one another.
But often did the crows caw,   225
Dividing among themselves the corpses.
And the jackdaws would speak in their own tongue,
As they flew out after prey.

Thus it was in ,those battles
And in those campaigns,
But such a battle as this   230
Had never been heard of before.

6

The Defeat of the Russians and the
Great Sorrow of the Russian Land

From early morning unto evening
And from evening unto morning
The tempered arrows fly.
Sabres ring against helmets   235
And kharalug lances crash
On an unknown plain
Amidst the Polovetsian Land.

And the black earth under horses' hooves   240
Was sown with bones,
And watered with blood,
And from these bones
There sprang up sorrow
Throughout the Russian Land.   245

What sound do I hear,
What rings in my ears,
Far away, early, before the dawn?
Igor turns back his troops;
He fears for his dear brother Vsevolod.[2]   250

They fought for a day,
They fought for another,
And on the third day, towards noon,
Igor's banners fell.

Here brothers were parted   255
   from one another,
On the shore of the swift-running Kayala.

2. The *Ipat'yevskaya Chronicle* tells that the Koui, Igor's Turkic mercenaries, were fleeing, that Igor tried to turn them back, and that Vsevolod was fighting so fiercely that "no weapon was left in his hand."

And here the blood-red wine ran out,
Here the brave Russians finished their feast:
Having brought their kin to drunkenness,   260
They themselves lay down
For the Russian Land.[3]

The grass bows in pity
And the trees, in sorrow,
Bend to the ground.   265

For now, O brothers,
A time of sorrow has come,
And desolation covers our troops.
Obida[4] has risen up
In the army of the grandson of Dazhbog.   270

As a maiden she stepped forth
Into the Troyan Land;[5]
With her swan's wings
She splashed the Blue Sea by the Don.
And, splashing, she banished   275
The times that were fat.

The wars of the princes
Against the heathen
Have ended.
For brother said to brother: 280
    "This is mine, and this too is mine."
And the princes began to say of small things:
    "This is great."
And they began, among themselves,
Discord to forge.   285

And the heathen, from all directions,
Came into the Russian Land in war.

O far has the falcon flown,
Killing birds, to the sea![6]
But Igor's brave army will not be raised!   290

Lamentation shrieks for it,
And Sorrow gallops through the Russian Land,
Hurling fire at the people from flaming horns.[7]

3. The battle is compared to a feast: the wine is the strength of the Russians which, although sufficient to intoxicate the enemy, was not enough to defeat him. The word translated "kin" is *svaty*; a *svat* is the father of one's son's wife or of one's daughter's husband. Many a Russian prince was married to a Polovetsian.
4. *Obida* (wrong, injustice, offense) is pictured as a maiden with swan's wings.
5. The Russian land.
6. Cf. lines 138—143. Igor is the falcon, the birds are the Polovetsians. Now the falcon has fallen, never to rise again.
7. A difficult and disputed passage. Many Russian families, upon hearing of the death of a male relative in the battle, lit traditional funeral fires. Sorrow (word of the death of a loved one) is personified as a warrior who hurls Greek fire at the Russian homes from horns (tubes) such as those used by the Greeks and Polovetsians in warfare (Adrianova-Peretts; Dmitriyev and Vinogradova).

And the Russian women wept, saying:
  "Now we cannot think of our dear husbands   295
    with our thoughts,
  Or dwell on them in our minds,
  Or gaze on them with our eyes.
  And gold and silver we shall never wear again."

And Kiev, brothers, groaned in its sorrow,   300
And Chernigov in its misfortune.
Sadness flooded the Russian Land,
Heavy sorrow flowed in the Russian Land.

But the princes continued to sow discord among themselves,
And the pagans roamed the Russian Land in war,   305
Taking as tribute from each cottage
A squirrel's skin.[8]

And so the two brave sons of Svyatoslav,
Igor and Vsevolod, by their willfulness
Awakened the evil that their father Svyatoslav,   310
The awesome Grand Prince of Kiev,
Had lulled by his might.[9]

He flailed with his mighty armies and kharalug swords.
He invaded the Polovetsian Land,
He trampled level the hills and ravines,   315
He muddied the rivers and lakes,
He dried up the streams and swamps.

Like a whirlwind he plucked the pagan Kobyak
From the midst of his great iron armies
At the bend in the sea.   320
And he was brought to Kiev city,
To the Hall of Svyatoslav's Retainers.[1]

Then the Germans and the Venetians,
The Greeks and the Moravians
Sang the praises of Svyatoslav.   325
Now, though pitying him,
They condemn Prince Igor:
For he sank his wealth

8. The chronicles report that as early as 859 the Varangians and the Khazars collected white squirrel skins as tribute.
9. Another disputed passage. The poet apparently reproaches Igor and Vsevolod for persisting in their quixotic campaign against the Polovetsians, a campaign undertaken without the support of the senior princes of Rus', such as Svyatoslav Vsevolodovich of Kiev. (Note that Svyatoslav was their cousin, not their father. He is called "father" because of his senior position.) This ill-conceived campaign was particularly reprehensible because Svyatoslav of Kiev had only recently "lulled by his might" the "evil" which was the power of the Polovetsians (see n. 1, below).
1. In 1183 Grand Prince Svyatoslav inflicted a terrible defeat on the Polovetsians, taking prisoner their Khan Kobyak and his sons, who were held in Kiev in the Hall of the Retainers (*gridnitsa*), a building where the prince met with his retinue.

To the depths of the Kayala,
  the Polovetsian river,   330
Pouring into it the gold of Russia.[2]

Now Prince Igor has given up his golden saddle
For the saddle of a slave.[3]
The walls of the cities have despaired
And gaiety languishes.   335

7

The Dream of Svyatoslav and His Talk with the Boyars

And Svyatoslav had a troubled dream
In Kiev, on the hills.[4]

"On the evening of that night
They clothed me," he said,
"In a black shroud, on my cedar bed.   340
They poured me blue wine mingled with bitterness.
From empty Polovetsian quivers
They sprinkled great pearls upon my breast,
And they treated me tenderly.[5]

"And across the golden ceiling   345
  of my tower chamber
There is no ridge-beam.[6]
And from evening through all the night,
Grey crows cawed
There at Plensk, along the river,   350
Where used to be the Kiyan thickets,
And then they flew off to the Blue Sea."[7]

And the boyars said to the Prince:
"Grief has taken your mind prisoner, O Prince.
Lo, the two falcons have flown   355
From the golden throne of their father
To seek for themselves the city of Tmutarakan',
Or drink with their helmets from the Don.

2. Igor's wealth and the gold of Russia are the men lost in battle.
3. According to the *Ipat'yevskaya Chronicle*, Igor was taken prisoner as he returned to the battle after his unsuccessful attempt to turn back the Koui.
4. The hills were the higher part of the city, above the river, where the grand prince lived.
5. Svyatoslav's dream contains a number of symbols, some clear, others not. The shroud suggests death, and the wine mingled with bitterness is the sorrow the prince must bear. The pearls are tears.

6. Absence of a ridge-beam is probably a sign of death. In pre-Christian days it was the custom to raise part of the roof so that Death might more easily enter and depart with the spirit of the dying person.
7. The verses beginning "And from evening" are obscure and perhaps defective; there are several plausible readings. Grey crows are associated with death and Plensk is taken to be a place in the Kiev district. The word *kiyan* (*kisan* in another ms.) is obscure.

"But the falcons' wings
Have been brought to the ground
By the swords of the pagans,
And the falcons themselves
Are bound in bonds of steel.   360

"Now it was dark on the third day:
The two Suns[8] grew dim,   365
Both crimson pillars burnt out,
And with them the two young Moons,
Oleg and Svyatoslav,[9]
Were clouded over with darkness
And sank into the sea,
And emboldened the men of Khinova.[1]   370

"On the river Kayala
Darkness shrouded the light.
And the Polovetsians spread
    across the Russian Land   375
Like a brood of leopards.

"Now shame has replaced glory
And thundering violence has stunned freedom;
Div has plunged to earth.[2]
And, lo, the beautiful Gothic maidens   380
Are singing on the shore of the Blue Sea:[3]
Jingling their ornaments of Russian gold,
They sing the praises of the days of Bus,[4]
And nurse the revenge of Sharukan.[5]

"But we, the retinue,   385
In vain do we seek joy."

8. Igor and Vsevolod. In the chronicles pillars of fire in the sky were often viewed as portents.
9. The name Oleg may be a copyist's error. At the time of the campaign Igor's son Oleg was only about ten years old. Perhaps he is named in error for Igor's older son Vladimir who, with Prince Svyatoslav Ol'govich of Ryl'sk, was taken prisoner by the Polovetsians.
1. The meaning of "men of Khinova" is unclear. Probably it was a general designation for the east, although it may refer to the Finns.
2. Earlier in the poem, Div—the bird of ill omen—warned the enemy of the Russians' approach. Now she has "plunged to earth," bringing misfortune to Igor.
3. As V. V. Mavrodin points out, Goths (or their descendants) were living on the Taman' Peninsula in the twelfth century. Since Igor's campaign was toward the Don and Tmutarakan' (Taman'), it threatened the Goths as well as the Polovetsians. Hence the rejoicing of Gothic maidens at the defeat of the Russians (Adrianova-Peretts).

4. The identity of Bus is uncertain. He may have been a Polovetsian khan of the eleventh century, but D.S. Likhachev suggests that he was a fifth-century prince of the Antes, Slavs living north of the Black Sea.
5. In the late eleventh and early twelfth centuries the very existence of the Kievan State was threatened by two Polovetsian alliances: one was led by Khan Bonyak the Mangy, the other by Khan Sharukan the Old. Sharukan himself had been captured by Svyatoslav in 1068. In 1107 Bonyak and Sharukan attacked Kiev again and were defeated. The Polovetsian offensive continued, however, and was finally defeated by the Russians under Vladimir Monomakh. Under the year 1185 (right after Igor's defeat but long after the death of Sharukan), the *Ipat'yevskaya Chronicle* reports these words of Khan Konchak (Sharukan's grandson) to Khan Gza: "Let us go against the Kievan Land, where our brothers and our Grand Prince Bonyak were defeated."

8

The Golden Word of Svyatoslav and His Appeals for Princely Unity

Then the Great Svyatoslav
Spoke a golden word,
Mixed with tears, and said:
"O my sons, Igor and Vsevolod!   390
Too soon did you torment the
Polovetsian Land with your swords
To seek glory for yourselves.
But with no glory to yourselves
Did you gain victory;   395
With no glory to yourselves
Did you spill the blood of the pagans.

"Your brave hearts were forged
 from strong steel
And tempered in daring.   400
But what have you done
 to my silver-grey hair!

"And I do not see the armies
Of my rich and mighty brother Yaroslav,[6]
With his multitude of warriors: 405
 With his Chernigov boyars,
 And with his commanders,
 And with his Tatrans,
 And his Shelbirs,
 And his Topchaks,   410
 And his Revugs,
 And his Olbers.[7]
They, without shields,
And with their daggers only,
With a shout do overcome whole armies,   415
Ringing out the glory of their fathers.

"But you said:
 'Let us take heart among ourselves.
 The glory of the past we too shall seize,
 And the glory of the future we shall share.'   420

"And is it indeed a marvel, brothers,
For an old man to become young again!
When the falcon loses his feathers

6. Svyatoslav wonders why his brother, Yaroslav, Prince of Chernigov, did not aid Igor. Or is he again upbraiding Igor for setting out on the campaign unsupported? Igor did in fact consult with Prince Yaroslav prior to the campaign, and the latter contributed his boyar Olstin Oleksich and some Turkic mercenaries (Koui) to Igor's army.
7. The Tatrans, Shelbirs, et al., were noble clans of the Koui.

He drives high the other birds,
And does not permit his nest to suffer wrong.[8]   425
But this is the evil:
The princes give me no aid;
The times are turned inside out."[9]

Lo, in Rimov, they cry out
Under Polovetsian sabres,   430
And Vladimir from his wounds.
Sorrow and anguish to the son of Gleb![1]

O Grand Prince Vsevolod!
Have you not thought to fly from afar,
To guard the Golden Throne of your fathers?[2]   435
For you can splash the Volga with your oars
And lade the Don with your helmets.
Had you been there, then
Would a female slave sell at a *nogata*
And a male at a *rezana*.[3]   440

Across the dry land
You can hurl living spears:
 the daring sons of Gleb![4]

You, wild Ryurik and David!
Is it not your golden helmets   445
That are floating in blood?
Is it not your brave warriors
Who, wounded by tempered sabres,
Scream like wild oxen on an unknown plain![5]

---

8. This passage is full of metaphors, some echoing those that have appeared earlier. The moulting falcon is the aging Svyatoslav, with his "silver-grey hair," who still desires to protect his nest.

9. Scholars disagree on where the "golden word" of Svyatoslav ends. Some prefer "The times are turned inside out"; others "son of Gleb," below. I have chosen the former.

1. After Igor's defeat, Gza and Konchak invaded Rus'. Gza attacked along the Seym River in Chernigov and Konchak invaded Pereyaslavl'. Prince Vladimir Glebovich of Pereyaslavl' was wounded defending his city, which did not fall to the Polovetsians. In withdrawing from Rus', Konchak laid waste the town of Rimov on the Sula River in Pereyaslavl'.

2. Grand Prince Vsevolod Yur'yevich Big Nest of Vladimir (r. 1177–1212) was the most powerful prince of Russia at this time. Son of Yuriy Dolgorukiy and grandson of Vladimir Monomakh, Vsevolod never "sat on the Golden Throne of his fathers," although both his father and grandfather reigned in Kiev.

3. Had Vsevolod participated in Igor's campaign the Russians would have taken so many captives that a male would have brought only a *nogata* and a female only a *rezana*, coins of little value.

4. The poet adds, rather as an afterthought, that Vsevolod could use the sons of Gleb as "living spears." The reference is to the sons of Prince Gleb Rostislavich of Ryazan' who were completely under Vsevolod's control.

5. Having chided Vsevolod for refusing to come to Igor's aid, the poet apostrophizes a number of other princes in his appeal for unity. Neither Ryurik Rostislavich of Smolensk nor his brother David took part in Igor's campaign. Yet, asks the poet, are not the men wounded in this campaign really the men of all the Russian princes? The idea of Rus' as one nation rather than a collection of principalities shines forth clearly in this passage.

Step then, lords, into your golden stirrups,   450
For the wrong of our times,
For the Russian Land,
   For the wounds of Igor,
       the wild son of Svyatoslav!

Prince Yaroslav Osmomysl of Galich!   455
High do you sit on your gold-bossed throne.
You propped the Hungarian mountains
With your iron armies,
Barring the path to the king,
Blocking the Danube gates,   460
Hurling supplies across the clouds,
Meting justice unto the Danube.

Fear of your might flows throughout the lands.
You force the gates of Kiev,
And from the Golden Throne of your fathers   465
You shoot at the sultan in a distant land.[6]
So, lord, shoot at Konchak, the pagan slave,
For the Russian Land,
   For the wounds of Igor,
       the wild son of Svyatoslav!   470

And you, wild Roman, and Mstislav!
Bold thoughts drive your minds to brave deeds.
High do you soar to these daring exploits,
Like a falcon sailing the winds:
But you would surpass the falcon   475
   In your daring.

For you have stout lads of iron
Under helmets of Latin steel:[7]

6. F. I. Pokrovsky suggests that Prince Yaroslav Vladimirovich of Galich (d. 1187) was called *osmomysl* ("eight thoughts," "eight designs," "eight intentions") because of the eight great feats enumerated in *Prince Igor*: propping the Hungarian (Carpathian) mountains, barring the path of the Hungarian king, blocking the Danube gates, transporting supplies great distances, meting justice as far as the Danube, possessing such power that fear of him "spread throughout the lands," forcing the gates of Kiev, and striking at the sultan in a distant land. Prince Yaroslav, the father-in-law of Igor, is an intriguing figure. Militarily powerful—his power apparently extended at one time to the Danube, to the borders of the Byzantine Empire—he nevertheless was long threatened by a pretender to his throne who had the support of the Grand Prince of Kiev. At one time Yaroslav did seize Kiev. The passage concerning shooting at the sultan in a distant land is puzzling. A. S. Orlov believes that the author of *Prince Igor* had heard of preparations for the Third Crusade against Sultan Saladin and of Yaroslav's intention to join that crusade.

In writing of Yaroslav's death, the *Ipat'yevskaya Chronicle* says: "And he was a prince wise and eloquent, and God-fearing, and honored in the lands and glorified in the armies."

7. The word *paporzi*, here translated "stout lads," is much disputed. Perhaps it should be translated "shoulder pieces of mail" or "shirts of mail." "Latin" steel means steel of western European manufacture.

The earth shook because of them,
And many lands   480
   Khinova, Lithuania,
   The Yatvyagi, the Deremela,
   And the Polovetsians[8]
Threw down their spears
And bowed their heads,   485
Under your kharalug swords.

But, O Prince,
For Igor the sun's light has dimmed
And the trees, to no good,
Have dropped their leaves.[9]   490
   Along the Ros',
   Along the Sula,
The towns have been portioned;[1]
But Igor's brave army will not be raised.

The Don calls you, O Prince,   495
And summons the princes to war;
For the sons of Oleg,
   Brave princes,
Have already done battle.

Ingvar and Vsevolod and all three sons of Mstislav: 500
Six-winged ones of a not bad nest![2]
Did you not gain your lands
By the fortunes of war?[3]
Then where now are your golden helmets,
And your Polish spears and shields?   505
Guard the gates of the plains
With your sharp arrows,
For the Russian Land,
   For the wounds of Igor,
     the wild son of Svyatoslav!   510

---

8. The Yatvyagi and Deremela were Lithuanian tribes. Roman Mstislavich (d. 1205) did indeed make war against the peoples mentioned. The Mstislav named here was probably Roman's cousin, Prince Mstislav Yaroslavich the Dumb (d. 1226) of Lutsk and Peresopnitsa.
9. The trees have lost their leaves because of Igor's defeat, or perhaps because of their sympathy for him. This is "to no good" (*ne bologom*), since it is May and trees should not be losing their leaves.
1. Among the victorious Polovetsians.
2. Ingvar and Vsevolod were princes of Lutsk, in Volynya. The three sons of Mstislav were Roman (see n. 8), Vsevolod, and Svyatoslav. "Six-winged ones of

a not bad nest" is a literal translation of a puzzling original. The reference again may be to falcons: the feathers of each wing of the falcon are divided into three parts (N. V. Sharleman).
3. The meaning of this passage is uncertain. The usual interpretation is: "You did not acquire your lands by the fortunes of war." But the Volynya princes were warlike and received aid from the Poles in their struggles against the Kiev and Galich princes. Adrianova-Peretts surmises that the interrogative particle *li* has been omitted from the passage by a copyist. Assuming the *li*, the translation given is possible and more satisfactory than the usual one.

For now the Sula no longer flows
With its streams of gold
For the city of Pereyaslavl';
And the Dvina flows as a swamp,
 To those dread men of Polotsk,   515
 To the shouts of the pagans.[4]

Alone did Izyaslav, the son of Vasil'ko,
Ring his sharp swords against the helmets of the Lithuanians,
Smiting the glory of his grandfather Vseslav,[5]
But was himself, on the bloodstained grass,   520
 under his red shields,
Smote by Lithuanian swords.
And, with his beloved on his couch beside him,
He said:
 "The birds, O Prince, have softly covered   525
 Your retinue with their feathers,
 And wild beasts have licked their blood."[6]

And his brother Bryachislav was not there,
Nor was the other, Vsevolod.[7]
Alone did he give up his pearly soul   530
 from his brave body,
Through his neckpiece of gold.[8]

Voices are saddened,
Mirth is wilted,
Trumpets do not blare   535
 in Goroden.[9]

O Yaroslav, and all the grandsons of Vseslav![1]
Lower your banners,

4. Even the rivers of Rus' are affected by Igor's defeat. The Sula no longer "flows with its streams of gold"; but one is impressed to read that the distant Dvina "flows as a swamp" as if to warn the men of Polotsk of danger, presaged by the shouts of the victorious Polovetsians. Or does the Dvina merely brings news to Polotsk of Igor's defeat, a defeat for all Rus'?

5. Izyaslav was the son of Prince Vasil'ko Svyatoslavich of Polotsk who died c. 1144. Izyaslav was the great grandson of Vseslav the Wizard.

6. The original of the phrase, dubiously translated "with his beloved on his couch beside him," is clearly defective. Further, is it Izyaslav who speaks? In his translation of *Prince Igor* into modern Russian, Aleksey Yugov puts these words into the mouth of Boyan the Bard. Cf. above, p. 30, "Or your song, Wise Boyan," etc.

7. Izyaslav's brother, Bryachislav Vasil'kovich, was Prince of Vitebsk. The other brother of Izyaslav was Vseslav, Prince of Polotsk. "Vsevolod" may be an error, or Izyaslav may have had a brother by that name.

8. According to Russian folk tradition, the soul resided in the throat, just above the breast bone and below the Adam's apple.

9. The original reads, "Trumpets blare in Goroden." I have followed S. K. Shambinago and V. I. Stelletskiy in assuming that the negative particle has been omitted. Cf. this passage with the one on p. 30: "Horses neigh beyond the Sula; / Glory rings out in Kiev. / Trumpets blare in Novgorod; / Banners flutter in Putivl'."

1. D. S. Likhachev believes that this passage should read, "O grandsons of Yaroslav and all the grandsons of Vseslav!" The descendants of Yaroslav the Wise of Kiev (d. 1054) and Vseslav Bryachislavich of Polotsk (d. 1101) long warred with one another.

Put away your blunted swords!
For you have already fallen from the glory of your grandfathers!   540
For with your sedition you began to bring
The pagans into the Russian Land,
    the patrimony of Vseslav.
In your discord violence came
    from the Polovetsian Land!   545

9

The Song of Vseslav

In the seventh age of Troyan,[2]
Vseslav cast lots for his beloved maiden.
Sustained by slyness he saddled his horse
And galloped to Kiev city,
And with his spear touched the Golden Throne of Kiev.   550

But he galloped away from Belgrad
As a wild beast, at midnight,
Shrouded in blue mist.

He snatched success on the third try,
And forced the gates of Novgorod,   555
Shattering the glory of Yaroslav.

And he raced as a wolf,
From Dudutki to the Nemiga.[3]

On the Nemiga
They scattered heads like   560
    sheaves of grain,
And threshed them with
    kharalug flails;
On the threshing floor
    they placed men's lives,   565
And winnowed their souls
    from their bodies.
On the bloody shores of the Nemiga

2. If the age of Troyan was the pagan, pre-Christian age of Russian history, then perhaps the "seventh age of Troyan" signified the end of the pagan era, just as the seventh day was the last day of Creation and was followed by the first day of the history of the world. But this interpretation is dubious.

3. Prince Vseslav of Polotsk tempted fortune in his bid to seize Kiev, the "beloved maiden." He had probably attacked Novgorod twice prior to his capture and burning of that city ("the glory of Yaroslav") in 1067. On March 3, 1067, Vseslav was defeated by Izyaslav of Kiev in a battle on the Nemiga River in Minsk District. Prior to the battle

Vseslav was encamped at Dudutki, identified as a small town near Novgorod (according to Karamzin) or as a village south of Minsk (according to Stelletskiy). Following the battle on the Nemiga, Izyaslav promised Vseslav peace and pardon, but instead seized him and his two sons and imprisoned them in Kiev. The next year the Kievans overthrew Izyaslav and proclaimed Vseslav their prince. But he ruled in Kiev for only seven months ("with his spear touched the Golden Throne"); Izyaslav returned with his ally King Boleslaw of Poland, and Vseslav fled, first to Belgrad (Belgorod), a town near Kiev, and then to Polotsk.

On the bloody shores of the Nemiga
The sowing was to no good:
They sowed the bones of Russian sons.[4]   570

Prince Vseslav judged the people,
And gave out cities to the princes;
But at night he loped like a wolf:
From Kiev he loped to Tmutarakan',
Arriving before the cock crowed,   575
Cutting the path of the mighty Khors.[5]

The bells of morning service
    rang for him in Polotsk,
Early, in Saint Sofiya,
And in Kiev he heard the sound.[6]   580
Though his wizard's soul was in a brave body,
Yet often did he suffer misfortune.
The wizard Boyan long ago sang of him wisely:
"Not the clever one,
Nor the skillful one,   585
Nor skillful bird,
Shall escape the judgment of God."[7]

O moan, Russian Land!
Recalling the earlier years
And the first princes!   590
One could not nail old Vladimir
    to the hills of Kiev!
But of his banners,
Some are Ryurik's, others are David's;
But their banners flutter apart,   595
And their spears sing.[8]

10

The Lament of Yaroslavna[9]

The voice of Yaroslavna is heard on the Danube:
An unseen cuckoo, she sings at dawn:

4. The poet compares the battle on the Nemiga to the peaceful work of the harvester and condemns in a dramatic and poetic fashion the internecine wars of the Russian princes. Neither the grandsons of Vseslav nor the grandsons of Yaroslav were victorious, but their warring weakened Rus'.
5. Outwardly an ordinary man, Vseslav was in truth a wizard. Khors was the pagan Russians' sun god.
6. The morning bells of Saint Sofiya in Polotsk (Vseslav's city) were rung for him and he could hear them in Kiev where he was held prisoner.
7. Likhachev suggests that the meaning of "Nor skillful bird" is "nor one who is skillful enough to fly like a bird."

Compare the Russian proverb, from the collection of Dal': "Neither the clever one, nor the skillful one, nor the miserable, nor the rich, shall escape God's judgment."
8. Vladimir I was often away on campaigns; he could not be kept in Kiev. His successors, however, such as the brothers Ryurik and David of Smolensk, although possessing the banners of old Vladimir, do not fight as one against the enemies of Russia. (In 1185 David had refused to join Ryurik in a campaign against the Polovetsians.)
9. Yaroslavna, Igor's second wife, was the daughter of Prince Yaroslav Osmomysl of Galich. Her Christian name was Yefrosiniya (Euphrosyne).

"I shall fly," she says,
"As a cuckoo, along the Danube.   600
I shall wash my sleeves of beaver
In the river Kayala.
I shall cleanse the bleeding wounds
On the mighty body of my prince."

Yaroslavna weeps at dawn   605
On the walls of Putivl', saying:
"O Wind, O Sailing Wind!
Why, O Lord, do you blow so strongly!
Why do you drive the arrows of Khinova
On your peaceful wings   610
Against the troops of my Beloved!
Is it not enough for you,
Flying on high beneath the clouds,
To rock the ships upon the Blue Sea!
Why then, O Lord, did you scatter   615
My happiness about the feather-grass!"

Yaroslavna weeps at dawn
On the walls of Putivl' city, saying:
"O Dnepr, Son of Renown!
You cut through the mountains of stone,   620
Through the Polovetsian Land!
You cradled the long boats of Svyatoslav
Till they reached the army of Kobyak.[1]
Then cradle, O Lord, my Beloved to me,
That I may not soon send my tears to him,   625
To the Sea."

Yaroslavna weeps at dawn
On the walls of Putivl' city, saying:
"O Bright and Thrice-Bright Sun!
For all you are warm and beautiful!   630
Then why, O Lord, did you send
Your hot rays onto the troops
Of my Beloved!
On the waterless plain,
Why did you warp their bows with thirst   635
And close their quivers with sorrow!"

11

Igor's Escape

The sea tosses at midnight,
The whirlwind comes in clouds.

1. Svyatoslav and his men traveled in long boats down the Dnepr in their campaign against the Polovetsians in 1184.

And God shows Prince Igor the way
From the Polovetsian Land,   640
To the Russian Land,
To the Golden Throne
  of his fathers.

The dusk of evening is gone:
  Igor sleeps,   645
  Igor wakes,
  Igor, in his thoughts,
    measures the plain
From the Great Don to the Little Donets.

And Ovlur[2] whistled beyond the river   650
  for a horse,
Warning the prince:
  "Prince Igor should not delay!"
Ovlur shouted, the earth shook,
The grass quivered, and the Polovetsian tents   655
  began to move.

And Prince Igor sped as an ermine
  to the rushes,
Like a white duck to the water.
He leapt on the swift horse   660
And leapt from it, like a grey wolf.
And he fled toward the bend of the Donets;
He flew like a falcon through the mists,
Killing geese and swans morning, noon and night.

If Igor flew like a falcon,   665
Then Ovlur ran like a wolf,
Shaking from himself the cold dew.
And both harrowed their swift horses.

And the Donets said:
  "O Prince Igor!   670
  Great is your praise,
  And great is the chagrin of Konchak
  And the joy of the Russian Land!"

And Igor said:
  "O Donets!   675
  Great is your praise,
  Who cradled a prince on your waves,
  Spreading out green grass for him
  On your silver shores;
  Clothing him with warm mists   680

2. Ovlur (Lavor in the Chronicle) was a Polovetsian who helped Igor escape. See
the Introduction, p. 8.

In the shadow of a green tree.
You watched over him
    As golden-eyes on your waters,
    As sea gulls on your waves,
    As black ducks on your winds."   685

"Not like this," he said,
"Was the river Stugna with its shallow flow,
Devouring foreign streams and currents,
And widening toward its mouth.
It bore away Prince Rostislav   690
And imprisoned him in the depths,
Near the dark shore.[3]
Rostislav's mother wept
For the youth, Prince Rostislav.
The flowers were despondent in pity,   695
And the trees, in sadness,
    bent to the ground."

It is not magpies that chatter!
It is Gzak and Konchak who pursue Igor!
Now the crows do not caw,   700
The jackdaws are silent,
And the magpies do not chatter.
Only the snakes slither.[4]
The woodpeckers, with their tapping,
Show the way to the river,   705
And the nightingales tell of the dawn
    with happy songs.

Gzak speaks to Konchak:
    "If the falcon flies to his nest,
    Let us shoot the little falcon   710
    With our gilded arrows."[5]

Konchak says to Gzak:
    "If the falcon flies to his nest,
    Let us entangle the little falcon
    With a beautiful maiden."

        715

3. In 1093 Prince Rostislav Vsevolodo-vich (brother of Monomakh) was drowned in the Stugna as he fled following a defeat by the Polovetsians. He was only twenty-four at his death. See above, pp. 14–15.

A. K. Yugov gives an interesting explanation of this passage: "The Stugna in the eleventh century was a border river whose southern bank was held by the Polovetsian Horde, and whose northern bank was held by Kievan Rus'. And so, when the Stugna flooded in spring (and Rostislav, in the words of the Chronicle, was drowned when the river overflowed at flood time), it took in for-eign waters, that is, waters from the Polovetsian bank, and became 'foreign in blood' and . . . betrayed the Russian prince" (quoted by Adrianova-Peretts, p. 182).

4. The birds do not betray Igor to the pagans. The snakes are a different matter—but they can only slither. (The original, "poloziye polzosha tol'ko" ["Only the snakes slither"], conveys a wonderfully creepy feeling.)

5. The two khans disagree as to what is to be done now that Igor has escaped. The falcon is Igor; the little falcon is Igor's son Vladimir, still a prisoner of the Polovetsians.

And Gzak says to Konchak:
"If we entangle him with a beautiful maiden,
We will have neither the little falcon
Nor the beautiful maiden;
And the birds will make war against us   720
On the Polovetsian Plain."[6]

12

Final Praise for Igor and His Men

Boyan and Khodyna, Svyatoslav's songmakers
From the olden times of Yaroslav,
And favorites of Oleg,[7] said:
"It is difficult for the head to be without shoulders   725
And the body to be without a head."
So is it for the Russian Land without Igor.

The sun shines in the sky!
Prince Igor is in the Russian Land!
Maidens sing on the Danube,   730
And their voices waft across the sea
    to Kiev.

Igor rides up the Borichev Slope
To the Holy Mother of God Pirogozhchey.[8]
The lands are happy,   735
The cities are gay.

Having sung a song to the old princes,
Then to the young ones sing:
"Glory to Igor Svyatoslavich,
To Wild Ox Vsevolod,   740

6. Khan Konchak suggests that Vladimir be married to a Polovetsian maiden. Khan Gzak replies that if Vladimir is married to a maiden, then both will be lost to the Polovetsians. (Three years later, in 1188, Vladimir did marry the daughter of Konchak and returned to Rus' with her and a child.) The birds are the Russians (falcons).

7. This passage is defective and very difficult. If my interpretation is correct, then Boyan and Khodynaya were bards at the court of Svyatoslav and, perhaps, at that of his father Yaroslav and that of his son Oleg. I am indebted to George J. Perejda for the novel suggestion that Boyan was in fact Harold Hardrada, king of Norway (1046–66). Harold, who served the Byzantine empress, Zoë, and resided in Kiev for a time, was the author of a love song similar to the lament of Yaroslavna, Igor's wife. For this and other valuable new insights into *Prince Igor*, see George J. Perejda, *"Beowulf* and *Slovo o Polku Igoreve*: A

Study of Parallels and Relations in Structure, Themes, and Imagery," Diss. University of Detroit 1973. Alexander Stepanov has suggested that Khodynya was the author of *Prince Igor* and was a bard of the court of Grand Prince Svyatoslav Vsevolodovich. See Rzhiga, Kuz'mina, and Stelletskiy, p. 364.

8. Borichev Slope (*Borichev vzvoz*) in Kiev was a path, or road, leading from the river, along which lay the lower part of the city (the *Podol*), up the hill to the center of the town where the idol of Perun, god of thunder, had once stood. With the coming of Christianity late in the tenth century, the idol was destroyed. In the twelfth century Grand Prince Mstislav, son of Monomakh, founded a church on this spot. It was named for an icon of the Virgin called Pirogozhchey, an icon that had been brought from Constantinople. See Stelletskiy and Timofeyev, pp. 212–213.

And to Vladimir Igorevich!
Health to the princes
And to their retinues,
Who fight for Christians
Against the armies of the pagans!
Glory to the princes and their retinues!"
Amen.

Prince Igor's Campaign
As Related in the
Ipat'yevskaya Chronicle

The chronicles are the most valuable sources for early Russian history. An almost yearly account of wars, political events, church affairs, portents, and vital statistics of members of the families of the princes, these documents were written in a moralistic tone befitting their authors: the monks of early Russia.

The earliest chronicle (called "Nestor's Chronicle" or, more recently, the "Primary Chronicle") was compiled in the Monastery of the Caves on the bank of the Dnieper near Kiev in the latter half of the 11th and the early part of the 12th centuries. Much of it was compiled by a monk named Nestor, who carried the account to 1111 or 1112—the date is not certain. The chronicle was then taken over by Sylvester, Hegumen (abbot) of the Monastery of St. Mikhail at Vydubichi, south of Kiev, who may have edited Nestor's work or added to it. The chronicle was then continued to 1117—again the date is not certain—by a person unknown, probably also a monk of the Monastery of the Caves.

A major part of the "Primary Chronicle" is the so-called "Tale of Bygone Years" which purports to relate world history from the time of the Flood. The "Primary Chronicle" also contains material from the Greek chronicler George Amartol, semi-historical traditional tales such as the "Baptism of Rus' under Vladimir," and other material.

The original of the "Primary Chronicle" has been lost. But it served as the basis for many other chronicles written, or copied, in other parts of old Russia. The oldest extant chronicle, or compilation of chronicles, is the *Lavrent'yevskaya Chronicle*, written in 1377 by "the poor, unworthy, and much-sinning slave of God, the monk Lavrentiy" in Suzdal', northeast of Moscow. It contains the "Primary Chronicle" and a continuation thereof to the year 1377. The *Ipat'yevskaya Chronicle*, named after the Ipat'yevskiy Monastery in Kostroma where it was found by the historian N. M. Karamzin early in the nineteenth century, was probably written in Pskov. It is based on materials originally written in the south, and is in three major sections: (1) the "Tale of Bygone Years"; (2) a record of the years 1118–1199; (3) a record of 1200–1292. The second section, which contains the account of Igor's campaign translated below, was compiled in the Monastery of St. Mikhail.

In the year 6693 [1185].[1] Working his salvation, the Lord gave a victory to the Russian princes, to Svyatoslav Vsevolodich and Grand Prince Ryurik Rostislavich[2] in the month of March on the 1 day.

1. See note 1, p. 1.
2. Svyatoslav was prince in Kiev. Ryurik Rostislavich, Grand Prince of Kiev, was the senior prince of his generation.

Though Ryurik permitted Svyatoslav to reign in Kiev, he himself retained the real power. Note that the Chronicle refers to Ryurik as "grand prince."

Learning that Konchak was fleeing, they sent after him Kuntuvdey with 6000 men.[3] The latter, pursuing, did not find him [Konchak], for beyond the Khorol [River] their tracks had melted.[4]

Now Svyatoslav and Grand Prince Ryurik accepted this victory with prayers to the holy martyrs Boris and Gleb,[5] and went, each to his own land, praising God in the Trinity: the Father, Son, and Holy Ghost.

Now Prince Yaroslav of Chernigov had not gone [on the campaign] with his brother Svyatoslav, for, he said: "I have sent my man Olstin Oleksich to them and I cannot set out against my own man."[6] With this, he refused his brother Svyatoslav.

But Igor said to Svyatoslav's man: "May God not grant that we refuse to go against the pagans. The pagans are the common foe of all of us."

Then Igor took counsel with his retinue as to where they might overtake Svyatoslav's troops.

And the retinue said to him: "O prince, you cannot, like a bird, overtake him by flying: Lo, this man came to you from Svyatoslav on Thursday and he left Kiev on Sunday.[7] Then how, O prince, can you overtake [Svyatoslav]?"

And Igor was not pleased that his retinue spoke to him thus. For he wanted to go across the plain, along the Sula [River].

And there was a great storm of freezing snow, so that his troops could not see where to go [even] in the daytime and unto evening. Because of this, nowhere could they find the way to follow after Svyatoslav.[8]

That same spring, Prince Svyatoslav sent Roman Nezdilovich with Berendichi against the pagan Polovetsians.[9] With God's help they took the Polovetsian camps, many prisoners, and horses, in the month of April, on the 21, even on Easter Day.

Then Prince Svyatoslav went to Karachev in the land of the Vyatichi on his business.

At that same time, Igor Svyatoslavich, the grandson of Oleg, set out from Novgorod [Seversk], in the month of April, on the 23 day, on Tuesday, taking with him his brother Vsevolod of Trub-

3. Kuntuvdey (Kun"tugdyy in the original) was the prince of the Torks (a Turkic people living in Rus,' also called the Chernyye Klobuki or "Black Cowls"), who were at this time allies of the Russian princes. Later Ryurik was forced to move against Kuntuvdey and subjugate him.

4. V. N. Tatishchev writes of this incident that "[Kuntuvdey] could not overtake them, for the snows had gone and the ground had frozen and it was impossible to make out their tracks at night" (*Istoriya rossiyskaya* [Moscow-Leningrad, 1962–68], III, 134).

5. See note 5, p. 16.

6. Prince Yaroslav Vsevolodovich of Chernigov, Svyatoslav's brother, had sent an envoy to negotiate with the Polovetsians and did not want to attack while his envoy was in the enemy's camp.

7. Novgorod-Seversk is about 150 miles northeast of Kiev.

8. Apparently Igor sent his men out after Svyatoslav despite their advice to the contrary.

9. Roman Nezdilovich was the voivode of Kiev. The Berendichi (Berendei) were Turkic allies of the Russians.

chevsk, and his nephew Svyatoslav Ol'govich from Ryl'sk, and Vladimir, his son from Putivl'. And from Yaroslav he asked the help of Olstin Oleksich, the grandson of Prokhor, and Chernigov Koui,[1] and thus they went about quietly gathering together their retinue. Indeed, their horses were very fat.

As they were going toward the Donets River at evening time, Igor looked up at the sky and saw the sun standing like the moon. And he said to his boyars and his retinue: "Do you see? What is this sign?" Now they looked and all saw, and they lowered their heads, and his men said: "O prince, lo, this sign is to no good."

And Igor said to his brothers and to his retinue: "No one knows the mysteries of God. God is the maker of this sign and of the whole world. And whether that which God does to us is for good or for ill, this too we shall see." And having said this, he forded the Donets and thus arrived at the Oskol River. And he waited two days for his brother Vsevolod, who was coming by another way from Kursk. And from there they went to the Sal'nitsa [River]. And here scouts who had been sent out to capture a prisoner came to them and, arriving, said: "We saw your enemies riding in readiness; now either go quickly or return home, for ours is not the time."

And Igor spoke with his brothers: "If we do not fight, but turn back, then our shame will be worse than death. But let it be with us as God grants."

And thus, taking counsel, they rode through the night.

And next day, Friday, advancing at the time of the noon meal, they came upon the Polovetsian armies. Now their [the Polovetsians'] camp had been forewarned; it was aroused and they had gathered, from small to large, and stood on the other side of the river Syuyurliy. And they [the Russians] deployed 6 regiments: Igor's regiment in the center; and on the right his brother Vsevolod's; and on the left his nephew Svyatoslav's; in front of him his son Vladimir's; and another regiment, Yaroslav's, that was with Olstin and the Koui; and also in front, a third regiment—archers who were taken from all the princes.

And thus did Igor array his troops, and he said to his brothers: "Brothers, this we have sought. Now let us advance!"

And thus they set forth toward them, placing their trust in God.

And, as they approached the Syuyurliy River, archers came out from among the Polovetsian regiments and let fly arrows at the Rus', and then galloped away. Now the Rus' had not yet crossed the river Syuyurliy before the Polovetsian forces, who were standing farther from the river, also galloped away.

Now Svyatoslav Ol'govich, and Vladimir Igorevich, and Olstin,

1. The Koui were Turkic people living in the Chernigov Land.

and the Koui, [and] the archers pursued them; but Igor and Vsevolod advanced cautiously, not permitting their regiments to disperse. Those Rus' who were ahead smote and took [prisoners].

The Polovetsians fled through their camp, and the Rus'—reaching the camp—took many prisoners.

Now the others returned at night to the camp with prisoners, and so were gathered together all the Polovetsians.

And Igor said to his brothers and to his men: "Lo, God with His strength has inflicted a defeat on our enemies and [has given] us honor and glory. Lo, we saw the Polovetsian armies that were many. But were they all gathered here? Let us ride the night, and those who come after us tomorrow, now if they all come, [only] the best horsemen will cross the ford, and with them and us it will be as God grants."[2]

And Svyatoslav Ol'govich said to his two uncles: "I have pursued the Polovetsians far and my horses are exhausted. If I set out now, then I shall merely be left behind on the road." And Vsevolod supported him, [arguing] that they should remain there.

And Igor said: "Brothers, it is no marvel for a man to die if he understands the reason." And they remained there.

As Saturday dawned, Polovetsian troops began to appear like a forest. The Russian princes were seized with consternation: who of them should go where? For there was such a numberless multitude of them [the enemy].

And Igor said: "Lo, knowingly, we have gathered to ourselves the whole land: Konchak, and Gza Burnovich, and Tokosbich Kolobich, and Etebich, and Tertrobich."[3]

And, dismounting from their horses, they took counsel. [Some] wanted to fight their way to the river Donets. They said: "If we flee we shall ourselves escape, but we will leave the black people.[4] That will be a sin against us from God, having betrayed them. Let us go: we shall either die or be alive in one place."

Having spoken thus, they dismounted from their horses and set out, fighting. And then Igor, by God's purpose, was wounded in the arm, and his left hand was deprived of its strength.

And there was great sadness in his army. And they had a voivode, and he had been wounded earlier.

And so they fought fiercely that day until evening, and many were wounded [and] many dead in the army of the Rus'. Saturday night came on and they went on fighting. It was dawn of Sunday [when] the Koui in the army panicked and fled.

2. Translation of the last part of this passage is uncertain. It appears that Igor wants to withdraw, although not all of his men are ready to leave with him. Igor is pictured as very human and not particularly heroic.
3. Polovetsian Khans.
4. The tax-paying lower classes; here, the common soldiers.

Now Igor was on his horse at this time, since he had been wounded. He set out toward their regiment, wanting to turn them back to the [other] regiments. Realizing how far he had gone from his men he took off his helmet [and] galloped back toward his troops because [he thought the deserters] had recognized their prince and were turning back. But then no one turned back; only Mikhalko Georgiyevich,[5] recognizing the prince, turned back. Now there were not many who fought well among the Koui, but there were a few simple [warriors] or some younger boyars.[6] For the good [fighters] were going on foot, and among them was Vsevolod [who] showed not a little courage. And as Igor was nearing his regiment, they [Polovetsians] rode across [his path] and there they seized him, at a distance of an arrow's flight from his regiment. Captured, Igor saw his brother Vsevolod fighting fiercely, and he asked for his soul's death that he might not see his brother fall. Vsevolod was fighting so fiercely that no weapon was left in his hand. And they were going in a circle near the lake.

And so, on the day of the Holy Resurrection, the Lord laid his anger upon us; in place of joy he laid upon us weeping, and in place of gaiety, bitterness, on the river Kayala.

And this is what Igor said: "I remembered my sins before the Lord my God: how I caused many killings and [much] bloodletting in a Christian land; how I showed no mercy to Christians, but took by storm the city of Glebov, near Pereyaslavl'. For then no little evil was done to guiltless Christians: fathers were separated from their children, brother from brother, friend from his friend, and women fom their husbands, and daughters from their mothers, and [female] friends from their friends, and all were thrown into the disorder of captivity. And there was sorrow then: the living envied the dead, the dead rejoiced like the holy martyrs who through fire overcame the temptations of this world; old men were crushed, youths suffered savage and merciless wounds; men were slashed and cut to pieces; women were defiled; and all this did I."

Igor said: "I was not worthy to live. And lo, now I see the vengeance of the Lord my God. Where now is my beloved brother? Where now is the son of my brother? Where is the child to whom I gave birth? Where are the boyars of my council? Where are my brave nobles? Where are my men of the line? Where are my horses and my priceless arms? Have I not been deprived of all these, and has not [the Lord] given me over as a captive into the hands of these godless ones? Lo, the Lord has repaid me for my lawlessness and for my evil. This day my sins have descended upon my head. The Lord is Truth, and His judgments are most righteous. For I

5. An otherwise unknown member of Igor's army. 6. Translation of this passage is doubtful.

have no part with the living. Lo, now I see other sufferings; taking the crown [of thorns], why did not I, who alone am guilty, take [upon myself] the suffering for all these? But, O Master, O Lord my God, do not reject me utterly! But as Your will is, O Lord, so is Your mercy toward us, Your servants."

And then, having finished [the battle], and the army being dispersed, each went to his own camp.

Now [Khan] Targa's man by the name of Chilbuk captured Igor, and Roman Gzich captured his brother Vsevolod; and Eldechuk of the Voburtsevichi, Svyatoslav Ol'govich; and Kopti of the Ulashevichi, Vladimir.

Then, on the battlefield, Konchak interceded for his *svat* Igor,[7] for he was wounded.

From so many men, few were saved, and these by chance. For it was impossible to escape by running, for the Polovetsian armies surrounded them like strong walls. But of our Rus' 15 men escaped, and of the Koui fewer, and the others were drowned in the lake.

At that time, Grand Prince Svyatoslav Vsevolodich had gone to Karachev and had gathered troops from the upper lands,[8] intending to go against the Polovetsians, to the Don, for the whole summer. As Svyatoslav was returning and was in Novgorod-Seversk, he heard from his brothers that they had gone against the Polovetsians, concealing themselves from him. And he was not pleased.

Now Svyatoslav went [down the Desna River] in boats, and so he arrived at Chernigov. And at that time there came running to him Belovolod Prosovich[9] and told Svyatoslav what had happened with the Polovetsians.

Hearing this, Svyatoslav sighed deeply, wiped away his tears, and said: "O my beloved brothers, and sons, and men of the Russian Land! God has given it to me to weaken the power of the pagans; but you, not restraining your youthfulness, have opened the gates to the Russian Land. May the Lord's will be done in all things. As I have grieved for Igor, so now I lament for Igor, my brother, even more."

Now after this, Svyatoslav sent his son[s] Oleg and Vladimir to the Posem'ye.[1] Hearing this, the Posem'ye cities were alarmed, and there was grief and wild sorrow such as had never been in the whole Posem'ye, and Novgorod-Seversk, and throughout the entire Chernigov Land: [their] princes had been captured, and the retinue cap-

7. Subsequently Igor's son Vladimir married Konchak's daughter. In the eyes of the chronicler, Igor was already *svat* to Konchak. A *svat* is the father or other relative of one member of a married couple in relation to the father or other relative of the other member.

8. The lands in the upper (southern) reaches of the Oka River.
9. Another Russian warrior who is not otherwise identified.
1. The lands along the Seym' River, a left tributary of the Desna.

tured [or] slaughtered. And there was seething, as in a churn; cities rose up, and no one had pity for his neighbor, but many then denied their souls, mourning for their princes.[2]

Then Svyatoslav sent to David of Smolensk[2] and said: "We have said: 'Let us go against the Polovetsians and spend the summer on the Don.' Now the Polovetsians have defeated Igor and his brother [and] his son. So go, brother, guard the Russian Land."

So David came down the Dnieper; and he, with other troops, stood at Trepol'.

And Yaroslav, in Chernigov, having gathered his troops, waited.

Now the pagan Polovetsians, having defeated Igor and his brothers, they acquired great audacity; and they gathered together their entire people [to invade] the Russian Land. But there was dissension among them. For Konchak said: "Let us go against the Kiev Land, where our brothers and our Grand Prince Bonyak were defeated."[3] But Gza said: "Let us go to the Seym', where the women and children have been left; gathered together they are ready prisoners for us. Let us seize the cities [for they are] without defense." And so they divided into two.

Konchak went to Pereyaslavl' and besieged the city and fought there for an entire day. Now Vladimir Glebovich, who was prince in Pereyaslavl', was bold and strong in battle. He rode out of the city toward them [the Polovetsians] and he charged them, but few of his retinue dared [follow] after him. And he fought with them fiercely, and many Polovetsians surrounded him. Then the others, seeing their prince fighting fiercely, dashed out of the city and thus rescued their prince, who had been wounded with three spears. Now this good Vladimir, wounded and suffering, rode into his city and wiped away the sweat for his fatherland.[4]

And Vladimir sent to Svyatoslav and to Ryurik and to David, and said to them: "Lo, the Polovetsians are at my gates. Help me!"

Now Svyatoslav sent to David, and David was standing at Trepol' with his Smolensk men. Now the Smolensk men started to hold a *veche*,[5] saying: "We have come as far as Kiev. If there had been war, we would have fought; but if we have to see another war, then we cannot, for we are exhausted."

Then Svyatoslav and Ryurik, with other relief forces, set out down the Dnieper against the Polovetsians, and David turned back with the Smolensk men.

Hearing this, the Polovetsians turned back from Pereyaslavl'; in passing, they besieged Rimov. The people of Rimov shut themselves

2. Brother of Grand Prince Ryurik Rostislavich.
3. See n. 5, p. 40.
4. Expressions involving the word *pot*, 'sweat,' are rather frequent in old Russian sources. It meant "labor, exploit, suffering."
5. A *veche* was a gathering of the people in Old Russia. Especially important in Novgorod (where princely power was not strong), it was not unknown in other parts of Rus'.

up in the city and crawled up onto the wall. Now, by God's will, two fortified sections of the city wall, with people, collapsed. And to the soldiers and other citizens there came terror, so that those citizens who fled from the city and fought, going about the Rimov swamp, avoided capture; but those who remained in the city, now these were all taken.

Now Vladimir sent to Svyatoslav Vsevolodovich and to Ryurik Rostislavich urging them to come to him, that they might aid him. But they delayed, waiting for David and his Smolensk men; and thus the Russian princes were late and did not overtake them.[6]

Now the Polovetsians, having taken Rimov city, made many prisoners and set out for their own land. And the princes returned to their homes. For they sorrowed, and with them their son Vladimir Glebovich,[7] for he had been badly wounded with mortal wounds, and [they sorrowed for the] Christians taken prisoner by the pagans. And lo, God, punishing us for our sins, brought the pagans upon us, not favoring them, but punishing us and turning us to repentance, that we might refrain from our evil deeds; and that, in punishing us by the presence of the pagans, we, submitting, might wake from our evil way.

Now the other Polovetsians went in another direction, to Putivl'. Gza had great forces, and, plundering the volosts,[8] they set fire to their villages. They also set fire to the outer defenses at Putivl', and returned to their own land.

Now Igor Svyatoslavich was at that time among the Polovetsians. And he said: "I, according to my worth, suffered defeat by Thy command, O Master [and] Lord, and it was not pagan insolence that destroyed the power of Thy slaves. I do not grieve in accepting, for my evil, all suffering: I have accepted all."

Now the Polovetsians, respecting his rank of voivode, did not do him [harm], but stationed with him 15 guards from among their sons, and from among the sons of their noblemen, five: all of them 20. But they gave him freedom: he rode where he wanted, he hunted with a goshawk. And 5 or 6 of his servants rode with him. And his guards obeyed him and respected him: where he sent one [there would he go, and] they would do, without objecting, that which he ordered. And he had brought a priest from Rus' for himself, with the holy service. For he knew not God's design, but it was

6. See n. 5, p. 42.
7. He was a "son" to the senior prince, such as Svyatoslav of Kiev, Ryurik, and David of Smolensk. Note that Ryurik and David were of the same generation as Vladimir of Pereyaslavl': Vladimir Monomakh was the great grandfather of all three. But Ryurik's and David's father (Rostislav Mstislavich) had been Grand Prince in Kiev, whereas Vladi-mir's father Gleb had been merely Prince of Pereyaslavl', a city that traditionally ranked third after Kiev and Chernigov in the ranking of Russian cities. Vladimir, who was born in 1157, died in 1187, perhaps as a result of wounds received in defending Pereyaslavl' against the Polovetsians.
8. That is, rural areas.

accomplished that he was to be there for a long time. But the Lord delivered him because of the prayers of Christians; for many sorrowed for him and poured out their tears for him.[9]

Now when he was among the Polovetsians, there was there a man, by birth a Polovetsian, named Lavor, and he had a good thought and said: "I shall go with you to Rus'."

Now at first Igor did not have faith in him, but kept to the high thoughts of his youth, although he had thought of taking a man and fleeing to Rus'. Now he said: "For the sake of glory I did not flee then[1] from my retinue, and now I shall not flee ingloriously."

Now there were with him a chiliarch's son[2] and his groom, and they incited him, saying: "Go, O Prince, to the Russian Land. If He wishes, God will deliver you." But a time such as he was looking for did not present itself.

But, as we were saying before: The Polovetsians were returning from Pereyaslavl', and to Igor his advisers said: "You have within yourself high thoughts, displeasing to the Lord. You seek to take a man and flee with him. But why do you not consider this: What if the Polovetsians return from the war? Now we have heard that they will kill the prince,[3] and you, and all the Rus'. Then you will have neither glory nor your life."

Now Prince Igor took their counsel to heart, fearing their [the Polovetsians'] coming, and he sought to flee.

But it was impossible for him to flee in the daytime, and at night guards guarded him. But just such a time he found, at the setting of the sun.

And Prince Igor sent his groom to Lavor, saying to him: "Cross to the other side of the Tor [River] with a bridled horse"; for he had decided to flee with Lavor to Rus'.

At that time, the Polovetsians had been drinking koumiss, and it was evening. His groom came and informed his prince, Igor, that Lavor was waiting for him. He arose, terrified and trembling, bowed down before God's icon and the Holy Cross, saying: "O Lord, who knows the hearts of men, save me, O Master, an unworthy one."

And putting on the cross and the icon, he stole away. Now his guards were playing and making merry, and the princes were feigning sleep.

Now reaching the river and fording it, he mounted the horse, and thus they went through the camps [of the Polovetsians].

Now the Lord worked this deliverance on Friday, in the evening,

9. Tatishchev wrote that many of Igor's countrymen gave liberally but "could not pay his ransom, for they [the Polovetsians] asked 2000 [grivna] for him, for the other princes 1000, and for the voivodes 200 or 100 grivna each" (p. 138).

1. During the battle.
2. The chiliarch's son was the lover of the wife of one of the khans and therefore knew of the Polovetsians' intentions (Tatishchev).
3. Igor's son, Vladimir? Perhaps the meaning is "[all] the princes."

and [Igor] went on foot for 11 days, to the city Donets, and from there he went to his own Novgorod. And they rejoiced in him.

From Novgorod he went to his brother, Yaroslav, in Chernigov, asking for aid [to go against] the Posem'ye. Now Yaroslav rejoiced in him and promised to give him aid.

From there Igor travelled to Kiev, to Grand Prince Svyatoslav, and Svyatoslav was glad [to see] him, as was his *svat*[4] Ryurik.

4. Concerning *svat*, see n. 7, p. 58. Svyatoslav's son Gleb was married to the daughter of Ryurik. Igor's son Svyatoslav was married to Yaroslava, daughter of Ryurik. Thus, Grand Prince Svyatoslav and Grand Prince Ryurik were *svat* to one another and Prince Igor and Grand Prince Ryurik were *svat* to one another.

Genealogy of Russian Princes

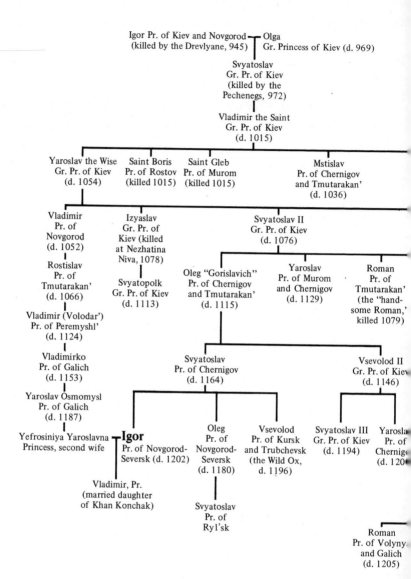

Igor Pr. of Kiev and Novgorod — Olga
(killed by the Drevlyane, 945) | Gr. Princess of Kiev (d. 969)

Svyatoslav
Gr. Pr. of Kiev
(killed by the
Pechenegs, 972)

Vladimir the Saint
Gr. Pr. of Kiev
(d. 1015)

Yaroslav the Wise   Saint Boris   Saint Gleb   Mstislav
Gr. Pr. of Kiev   Pr. of Rostov   Pr. of Murom   Pr. of Chernigov
(d. 1054)   (killed 1015)   (killed 1015)   and Tmutarakan'
                                                               (d. 1036)

Vladimir   Izyaslav   Svyatoslav II
Pr. of   Gr. Pr. of   Gr. Pr. of Kiev
Novgorod   Kiev (killed   (d. 1076)
(d. 1052)   at Nezhatina
                    Niva, 1078)
Rostislav
Pr. of   Oleg "Gorislavich"   Yaroslav   Roman
Tmutarakan'   Svyatopolk   Pr. of Chernigov   Pr. of Murom   Pr. of
(d. 1066)   Gr. Pr. of Kiev   and Tmutarakan'   and Chernigov   Tmutarakan'
                    (d. 1113)   (d. 1115)   (d. 1129)   (the "hand-
Vladimir (Volodar')   some Roman,"
Pr. of Peremyshl'   killed 1079)
(d. 1124)

Vladimirko   Svyatoslav   Vsevolod II
Pr. of Galich   Pr. of Chernigov   Gr. Pr. of Kiev
(d. 1153)   (d. 1164)   (d. 1146)

Yaroslav Osmomysl
Pr. of Galich
(d. 1187)   Oleg   Vsevolod   Svyatoslav III   Yaroslav
                           Pr. of   Pr. of Kursk   Gr. Pr. of Kiev   Pr. of
Yefrosiniya Yaroslavna — Igor Novgorod-   and Trubchevsk   (d. 1194)   Chernigov
Princess, second wife   Pr. of Novgorod- Seversk   (the Wild Ox,   (d. 120
                         Seversk (d. 1202) (d. 1180)   d. 1196)

                                           Svyatoslav
Vladimir, Pr.   Pr. of
(married daughter   Ryl'sk
of Khan Konchak)
                                                                       Roman
                                                                       Pr. of Volyny
                                                                       and Galich
                                                                       (d. 1205)

Genealogy of Russian Princes
who figure in the poem

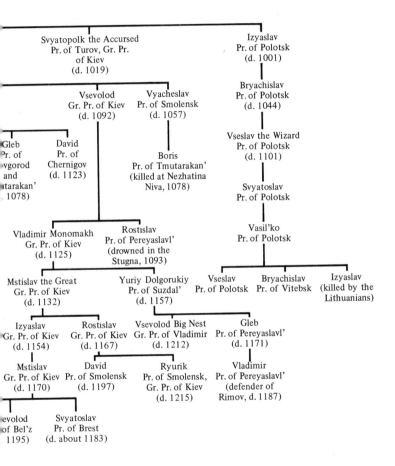

Selected Bibliography

I have relied primarily on the following works in preparing this book. The bibliography on PRINCE IGOR is immense, and many fine works in Russian, English, and other languages are available to those who wish to study the poem.

Adrianova-Peretts, V. P. "Slovo o polku Igoreve" i pamyatniki russkoy literatury XI–XIII vekov. Leningrad: Izdatel'stvo "Nauka," 1968.

Dmitriyev, L. A., and V. L. Vinogradova. Slovo o polku Igoreve. Leningrad, 1952.

Ipat'yevskaya letopis'. 1908; rpt. Moscow: Izdatel'stvo vostochnoy literatury, 1962.

Lavrent'yevskaya letopis' i Suzdal'skaya letopis' po akademicheskomu spisku. 1926; rpt. Moscow: Izdatel'stvo vostochnoy literatury, 1962.

Likhachev, D. S. Russkiye letopisi i ikh kul'turno-istoricheskoye znacheniye. Moscow-Leningrad: Izdatel'stvo Akademii nauk SSSR, 1947.

Orlov, A. S. Slovo o polku Igoreve. 2nd ed. enl. Moscow-Leningrad: Izdatel'stvo Akademii nauk SSSR, 1946.

Peretts, Volodimir. Slovo o polku Igorevim, pam'yatka feodal'noi Ukraini-Rusi. Kiev, 1926.

Rybakov, B. A., and S. A. Pletneva, eds. Istoriya SSSR. Vol. I. Moscow: Izdatel'stvo "Nauka," 1966.

Slovo o pl"ku Igoreve, Igorya syna Svyatoslavlya, vnuka Ol'gova. Ed. V. F. Rzhiga and S. K. Shambinago. Moscow: Gosudarstvennoye Izdatel'stvo khudozhestvennoy literatury, 1959.

Slovo o polku Igoreve. Poeticheskiye perevody i perelozheniya. Ed. V. Rzhiga, V. Kuz'mina, and V. Stelletskiy. Moscow: Gosudarstvennoye Izdatel'stvo khudozhestvennoy literatury, 1961.

Stelletskiy, V. I., and L. I. Timofeyev. Slovo o polku Igoreve. Drevnerusskiy tekst i perevody. Moscow: Izdatel'stvo Prosveshcheniye, 1965.

Vernadsky, George. Kievan Russia. New Haven: Yale University Press, 1948.

Yeremin, I. P., and D. S. Likhachev. Khudozhestvennaya proza Kiyevskoy Rusi XI–XIII vekov. Moscow: Gosudarstvennoye Izdatel'stvo khudozhestvennoy literatury, 1957.